The Anger of Stephen Crane

*—Say, when I planted those
hoofs of mine on Greek
soil I felt like the hull
of Greek literature. . . .*

CRANE

Chester L. Wolford

The Anger
of
Stephen Crane

Fiction and
the
Epic Tradition

University of Nebraska Press

Lincoln and London

Publication of this book was assisted by a grant
from the National Endowment for the Humanities.

The paper in this book meets the guidelines for
permanence and durability of the Committee on
Production Guidelines for Book Longevity
of the Council on Library Resources.

Library of Congress Cataloging in Publication Data

Wolford, Chester L., 1944-
The anger of Stephen Crane.

Includes bibliographical references and index.
1. Crane, Stephen, 1871–1900 – Criticism and
interpretation.   2. Epic literature – History and
criticism.   3. Classical literature – History and
criticism.   I. Title.
PS1449.C85Z983   1983   813'.4   82-8491
ISBN 0-8032-4717-6   AACR2

For Florence Lankard Wolford and Chester Wolford, Sr.

Preface

This is a study of Stephen Crane's use of and place in the continuing epic tradition. It focuses on the epic as a tradition and a genre: a tradition that recurrently destroys and recreates history and value, and a genre that at its best effectively reflects historical and evolutionary changes in consciousness. The book assumes that the epic did not die with Milton, but that because changes in consciousness occur neither with regularity nor often within a century or so of each other, epic time must be considered in terms of centuries or even millennia. It also assumes that the impulse to write epic continues and that some of the generic formulae of epic have been absorbed by the novels and poetry of romanticism and romanticism's progeny, among which must be included naturalism, existentialism, modernism, and postmodernism, among many other "isms" attributed to Crane: symbolism, impressionism, and nihilism. Stephen Crane was part of the process, and more than chronologically, his work lies somewhere between Milton's and the next great epic that awaits a talent able to encompass and express the change in consciousness that is to follow what Tillyard called the "world picture" and Stevens the "supreme fiction" of rational Christianity.

Stephen Crane attempted to repudiate the Christian-Miltonic vision and in direct proportion to his success he became what H. G. Wells called "the first expression of the opening mind of a new period."[1] Crane was not quite the first—Whitman, Melville, and others have some prior claims—but Crane does stand out as one who significantly widened the aperture of that "opening period."

In order to be one of the "first expressions" of a new period, especially in an epic sense, Crane needed to do two things: (1) be aware of, use, and finally reject former supreme fictions and notions of heroism, and (2) attempt to extend that tradition towards a new consciousness and new heroic ideals. Crane's epic task was to perceive, deal with, and express a new consciousness in a world seen as abandoned by God and beginning to be replaced by a scientifically modern, but essentially Lucretian world composed only of matter and void, a world without myths and such related imaginative constructs as history. Such a vision naturally produced great fear, despair, and even nihilism in those strong enough to deny the solace of the God-centered universe in which they had been raised to believe. Few were as strong as Crane, for few were as terrified and as able to persevere.

Enough has been written on the history of consciousness, mostly stemming from Jung's scattered comments, that I need not elaborate beyond saying that the epic tradition reflects that history, and reminding readers that the epic has been a traditional and most spacious vehicle through which changes in consciousness have been chronicled in the West. Joan Webber's *Milton and His Epic Tradition* (1979) is an excellent investigation of what she calls the "epic of consciousness."[2] This study owes much to Webber's book.

If certain views may be simplified and still be true, such may be the case in saying with Bowra that the history of Western consciousness reflects a consciousness that has expanded with respect to both space and time.[3] Western consciousness moves from Homer's hero-centered society to Virgil's group-centered empire to Dante and Milton's God-centered universe. Every period is influenced by these fictions, but not every period produces a consummate expression of a dominant fiction. Because an established fiction dominates society while a new one is gathering strength, even a period of great change such as the nineteenth century may not extend the tradition significantly. The old fiction must be sufficiently repudiated before a new one can take its place.

Epic repudiates and Stephen Crane repudiates.

Epics forge expressions of new fictions and Stephen Crane attempted to forge one.

Consequently, the subject is twofold: first, to see to what degree Crane was influenced by the formal epic tradition and how he set about repudiating it; second, to determine where and in what direction Crane broke new ground. My method is first to demonstrate the enormity of Crane's rejection of the Christian vision along with the nationalism and collectivism so successfully created on a large scale by Rome. Next I argue that Crane, in spite of his youth and his reputation even today among some critics and readers as an amazingly lucky and semiliterate genius, was extremely knowledgeable about the epic tradition and capable of working within it.

The discussion of epic conventions in Crane has been preceded by four articles. Warren D. Anderson's 1964 article, "Homer and Stephen Crane," is seminal to this book in associating some of Crane's literary devices with epic trappings and conventions in *The Red Badge*.[4] Anderson, however, errs in dismissing the Homeric notion of *areté*—striving toward excellence, often at any cost—as having much to do with Henry Fleming's character in particular or with *The Red Badge* in general, preferring to concentrate on *menos*, the Homeric Greek battle rage. Four years later Robert Dusenbery covered much the same ground in "The Homeric Mood in *The Red Badge of Courage*."[5] Donald Gibson wrote not only the excellent *The Fiction of Stephen Crane*, but also a note on the Cheery Man in *The Red Badge* as a *deus ex machina* and as part of that tradition of gods helping heroes.[6] Sister Mary Anthony Weinig's

"Heroic Convention in 'The Blue Hotel,'" suggests that Scully's home had a social structure much like that of Homeric households.[7]

There are numerous things I do not feel required to do. First, I think that I need not demonstrate once again that prose is an acceptable medium for writing in the epic tradition. Nearly all great novelists from Fielding to Joyce and beyond have proved it, and Ian Watt's *The Rise of the Novel* has become a critical assumption. When I discuss Crane's fiction in terms of techniques generally considered to belong to poetry, I also make no apology, for Daniel Hoffman's *The Poetry of Stephen Crane* (1956) has shown conclusively that Crane's fictional methods are "essentially those of poetry," a fact later supported by Frank Bergon's excellent *Stephen Crane's Artistry* (1975).[8]

I also believe that while "Fiction and the Classical Tradition" may have been a more technically accurate title for this study, "Fiction and the Epic Tradition" is more fundamentally correct. If by "classical" is meant what it means for Gilbert Highet in *The Classical Tradition* (1949)—the "literary patterns which we use: tragedy and comedy, epic and romance"[9]—it is also true that epic is such an "encyclopedic" genre, to use Frye's term, that comedy and most elements of tragedy may be subsumed in it.[10] Long before *Anatomy of Criticism*, Aristotle's *Poetics* goes on at some length showing how tragedy and comedy may be part of epic. Moreover, even when Crane pointedly employs classical tragedy or comedy, as in "The Blue Hotel" and "The Bride Comes to Yellow Sky," he just as pointedly includes not only epic trappings but also a certain epic breadth of theme as well. "Epic" is probably a better term here than "classical."

It is customary these days not to focus an entire chapter on one work, but *The Red Badge of Courage* is so completely epical that any discussion of it would dominate any chapter in which it appeared. As a result I have confined to a single rather extensive chapter a somewhat chronological reading of the novel. I have used the Virginia edition rather than Binder's edition in the *Norton Anthology of American Literature* (1979) not because the former is better but rather because all of Crane is conveniently available in that edition.

Two chapters chronicle Crane's fictional uses of such genres as tragedy and comedy. While both *Maggie* and *The Monster* use tragic structures, the former fails. Although drawing upon classical myth, *Maggie* does not employ epic to lend true tragic stature to the protagonist. *The Monster*, a product of Crane's maturity, to the extent that he had one, succeeds as a tragedy with epic significance. "The Bride Comes to Yellow Sky" and "The Blue Hotel" may be seen as comic and tragic epics of the American West. The final chapter summarizes Crane's accomplishments and speculates on some of his failures. Altogether, the chapter suggests that Crane's attempts to advance the tradition by searching out a new supreme fiction are on the same line that stretches from Whitman to Stevens and beyond—those writers who are attempting not only to decreate the imagination, but also to find a supreme fiction in the unmediated apprehension of the material world.

It should be noted here that "decreation" and "unmediated apprehension" have much in common with impressionism. All three concern themselves with representing reality in a strictly sensual manner. And while Crane has been called an impressionist from the beginning of his career, only in the last couple of decades has his impressionism been linked significantly with modes of consciousness. Among the more important treatments of Crane and consciousness have been Sergio Perosa's "Naturalism and Impressionism in Stephen Crane's Fiction," originally published in 1964, and a number of studies since that time, including those of Stallman, Gibson, Gullason, Katz, La France, Holton, Cazamajou, Levenson, Bergon, and Nagel.[11] Because my argument is so broad in its examination

of the broadest of genres as it applies to Crane, the threads of
these critics' arguments form much of the fabric of this one; it is
consequently impossible even to attempt to cite them often
enough. Nevertheless, it is appropriate to acknowledge that R.
W. Stallman's three decades of Crane scholarship have increased our knowledge of Crane exponentially. This book
owes much to Stallman and to Milne Holton's *Cylinder of
Vision*, the first study to yoke Crane's impressionism and
nihilism. Because in one way or another these and other critics
were able to demonstrate that Crane's vision was impressionistic, it became an easier task to apply the epic tradition to
Crane's impressionism and to its effects on Crane's rendering
of consciousness in much of his work. These critics are also
important for pointing toward Crane's last works, where he
seems to go beyond impressionism, even in the midst of
debilitating illness and financial trouble and much bad writing,
toward a style in which he abandons "objectivity" in favor of
rendering subjective responses impressionistically, a movement in which may lie more than a few seeds of postmodernism.

This book runs counter to at least two common critical
assertions about Crane's work. One is that Crane exalted the
group and felt that only by subsuming one's identity in some
human society larger than the self could one find contentment
or salvation. This view is bounded on one side by the balanced
and perceptive notions of critics like R. W. Stallman who
would make of Crane a lost Christian pilgrim in search of the
true faith. Such critics also have been among the first to point
out that Crane never found that faith. Crane pursued truth as
only an American puritan could, but his search was actively anti-Christian. At the other extreme lie those like "M. Solomon" who would make of Crane a disciple of Marx or Mar-
garet Fuller.[12] Such a view fails utterly to see the pervasive
irony in Crane, the bestiality of mobs in *The Whilomville Stories*

and *Maggie*, the cowardice of the group in "The Blue Hotel" and *The Monster*, and the blindness of the regiment in *The Red Badge* or any other of his war stories. "I was a Socialist for two weeks," he once said, "but when a couple of Socialists assured me that I had no right to think differently from any other Socialist and then quarreled with each other about what Socialism meant, I ran away."[13]

In short, to the degree that Crane was existential, he was so in a Kierkegaardian sense, and to the degree that he was a puritan, he partook of the puritan belief in the necessity of the lonely quest. Moreover, and from another point of view, Crane's distaste for the group can be seen as thoroughly bourgeois. Along with many contemporaries, Crane often betrays great anxiety about what Fredric Jameson calls "the primal nineteenth-century middle-class terror of the mob."[14] Naturalism may then be seen from this somewhat Marxist angle as another capitalist device for keeping the proletariat in its place. Still, these views were often actively, even violently, opposed to the instinct of the herd.

That Crane betrays naturalistic leanings is indisputable; that he may be explained adequately through his naturalism is not. Notions associated with literary naturalism—that man has little free will and is bound by heredity and environment; that values such as morality, choice, heroism, cowardice, and the like have little relevance—do not explain Crane. Naturalism was as vital a force in late nineteenth-century America as was tragedy for a couple of generations in ancient Greece, but just as no one seriously tries to explain Sophocles fully by calling him a tragedian, neither does naturalism adequately explain Crane. For example, Crane's protagonists are unlike the usual naturalistic protagonist. As Holton suggests, Crane's protagonists after Maggie seem bound by no rules of heredity and environment.[15] At least such rules are irrelevant to Crane's purposes. Many of his protagonists are so isolated from their environments that they have little in common with McTague: Maggie, a flower that "blossomed in a mud puddle"; outlaw Scratchy Wilson facing down an unarmed and married lawman; the mild, frightened Swede, an urban tailor, tearing the seams out of a rural Nebraska blizzard; farmboy Henry Fleming in the holocaust of the Civil War; Trescott, the honorable individual, struggling vainly in a dishonorable community; and a newspaperman rowing for his life in a fourteen-foot dingey on heavy seas.

The idea with which Crane is most often associated—that the fact of organic existence ("Sir, I exist!") does not create a sense of obligation in the universe—is not a notion of naturalism alone. It is also Epicurean. In fact, Lucretius is more similar intellectually to Crane than either Homer or Virgil. Lucretius is more able to celebrate the fact of a materialistic universe than is Crane, especially in the first few books of *De rerum natura*, his unfinished epic. When in book 6 Lucretius turns unflinchingly to describe the plague in Athens, the effects are remarkably similar to Crane's descriptions of death in war: both have seen the horror. Lucretius may have not only rivaled Homer and Virgil, but even exceeded them in Crane's mind. Nevertheless, once past the all-too-human gods, such a view is not entirely un-Homeric. "A Man Said to the Universe," as well as most of Crane's other works, owes as much to classical antecedents as it does to Howells, Garland, and Zola. The dark side of Crane, which is at least as pessimistic as the visions of Norris and other naturalistic writers, is not much darker than the vision that caused the shade of Achilles, who when alive was the vibrant symbol of human glory, to suggest that he would rather be a slave and alive than Achilles dead.

I hope in this book to connect Crane with that ancient vision and with the genres that shaped its expressions.

Acknowledgments

To acknowledge all contributions to this work would be impossible; too many contributed much. Eight people were particularly generous with their time, knowledge, and kindness: Milne Holton, Keith Fort, Wil Jewkes, and Harrison Meserole proved that professionalism is not incompatible with friendship. Roy Harvey Pearce single-handedly revived my interest in a dusty manuscript. Fred Crawford blue-penciled an early draft with a loving lack of mercy. R. W. Stallman lent many of his considerable resources during a difficult time. Norma Hartner typed and retyped the manuscript with unflagging cheerfulness.

I am grateful to the National Endowment for the Humanities for a grant to pursue research on Crane and postmodernism.

My children, Reeve and Rebecca, deserve much credit for possessing understanding beyond their years.

Most of all, to Gretchen Vanneman Wolford, for her intelligence and patience, I owe nearly everything.

Where are the beginnings of this epic impulse,
this impassioned quest for a Supreme Fiction?
The origins lie deep in the national psyche.
. . . There is one side of the American
character that shouts: throw over all tradition,
cut off the past, start and build anew; but
there is a counterpart that whispers: take all
tradition as yours, connect firmly with the
past, build the new only on the old.

JAMES E. MILLER, JR.

The American Quest for a Supreme Fiction

Chapter One

Enormous Repudiations and the Epic Impulse

Stephen Crane's life and art are mirrors for two sides of the American psyche: that which cries for novelty and the more acquisitive, which tells us to seize the old, use it, and make it ours. Like many Americans, Crane rejected the past with one hand yet clasped it to himself with the other, a seemingly paradoxical characteristic expressed in his lines on tradition:

> Tradition, thou art for suckling children
> Thou art the enlivening milk for babes;
> But no meat for men is in thee.
> Then—
> But, alas, we are all babes.[2]

If tradition is mere pabulum for "suckling children," and therefore to be rejected because it contains "no meat for men," it is also true, as Crane next acknowledges, that "alas, we are all babes." As Crane spent his life attempting to be courageous, to "be a man," as used to be said, his most dramatic efforts on behalf of this ironical condition lay on the side of rejecting the past. By all accounts these efforts were immense.

Repudiations
H. G. Wells wrote correctly of Crane's "enormous repudiations," for at one time or another Crane rejected nearly everything that was passively accepted by his family, his culture, and humanity in general. His mother's side of the family, the

Pecks, had among its number a dozen or so Methodist ministers, mostly of the hellfire and brimstone variety, although
Jesse T., Stephen's uncle, gained the respectability of a bishop-
ric. Many, including Crane's mother and father, were prolific
composers of tracts, pamphlets, articles, and even books,
often filled with flatulent bombast.[3] It was characteristic of
Stephen to reject this brand of denominational puritanism
very early: "I used to like church and prayer meetings when I
was a kid but that cooled off and when I was thirteen or about
that, my brother Will told me not to believe in Hell after my
uncle had been boring me about the lake of fire and the rest of
the side shows."[4] Thomas Beer says that Crane later went so
far as to tell a friend that "men had been allowed to pervert the
teachings of Christ and Buddha into formulae and there was
no such thing as sin 'except in Sunday school.'"[5] And Berryman quotes an exchange between young Crane and a psychology professor at Syracuse, an exchange that demonstrates well
Crane's rejection of orthodox Christianity. Reproving the
young man on horseback for bohemian activities, the professor is supposed to have said, "Tut, tut, what does Saint Paul
say, Mr. Crane?" Stephen reportedly answered, "I know what
Saint Paul says, but I disagree with Saint Paul."[6]

When Crane wrote to Nellie Crouse, "I detest dogma," he
meant dogma of any kind—religious, social, historical.[7] In
particular, he disliked the American democratic ideal which
supposes that the mass should rule in everything, a predilec-
tion for mob decisions that de Toqueville labeled the "tyranny
of the majority." Protestantism and patriotism blended into
Americanism in the second half of the nineteenth century and
for Crane became identified with and personified by "middle-
aged ladies of the most aggressive respectability."[8] Crane
hated them and what they stood for and called them "feminine mules," "hunks of women who squat on porches of
hotels in summer," who, like Martha Goodwin in *The Monster*,

were "the mausoleum of a dead passion."[9] In general, Crane was disgusted by the middle class and felt much more at home either in slums or palaces; Stallman quotes Crane's friend Harvey Wickham as saying that "with the middle class" Crane "was always a little David throwing stones at the collective Goliath."[10]

Such attitudes proved so deeply seated that they carried over into his art. When, for example, Crane attempted to write a novel about middle-class manners, as in *The Third Violet*, two things became clear: first, that his best portraits as well as his most admirable characters are the simple farmer and the heiress; and second, that he probably should have left writing for the middle class about the middle class to his friend and benefactor Howells. On the other hand, when Crane decided to pillory the middle class, as in *The Monster*, he succeeded brilliantly; and the companion pieces, "An Experiment in Luxury" and "An Experiment in Misery," whatever their merits as experimental fiction, represent societies in which Crane felt most at home, or at least in which he fancied himself to be most interestingly engaged.

Crane's most fervent hatred, however, was reserved for the bestiality of the mob. When facing the "collective Goliath," Crane generally held himself aloof. "He held aloof, too," continues Wickham, "when an indignant undergraduate mob hanged a certain unpopular student in effigy. He was rather given to holding aloof, especially if the animal was manifesting its capacity for collective action." In spite of much criticism to the contrary, Crane rejected the notion of "brotherhood," especially when it implied a passive sense of collective superiority, as in *The Sullivan County Tales and Sketches*, *Maggie*, and several Asbury Park or war reports, or when expressed in mob action, as in *The Red Badge* and "The Blue Hotel." Responding to a question about mob courage, Crane said: "The mob has no courage. That is the chatter of clubs and writers."[11]

Crane is a rare figure in American literature in that he belongs neither to that tradition which lauds individualism if it means praising captains of industry, nor to that which believes socialistic reform to be a cure for America's ills. He rejected the socialistic movement which was growing in late nineteenth-century America, yet he had no particular love for some of the more firmly entrenched capitalistic traditions. While Garland and Norris and Dreiser railed against the abuses of capitalism, and while Pound, Hemingway, and Mailer were later to damn collective mediocrity, Crane kept a wary eye out for both. His sketches are filled with a muted bitterness against the more cannibalistic aspects of capitalistic industrialism as well as against those who blindly accepted a losing throw of the dice. On one hand, for example, he could say that a certain "cowardice" lay at the root of Bowery life,[12] and on the other he could espouse unionism when such a view was almost universally (and always officially) opposed: "When I had studied the mines and the miner's life underground and above ground, I wondered at many things but I could not induce myself to wonder why the miners strike and otherwise object to their lot."[13]

Crane's distrust is not quite equally divided between the individual and the group, for while he distrusts individualism, he seems to have preferred it in his life as well as his fiction to the bestiality of collective action. Mankind manifests this bestiality in many of his stories, from the four foolish men in his early "Sullivan County Sketches," through the tribal Bowery gods of *Maggie*, the "mysterious fraternity" of *The Red Badge of Courage*, the ultimately repugnant community of *The Monster*, the conspirators of "The Blue Hotel," the Greek mob in his report called "The Man in the White Hat," to the mob of children in the very late "Whilomville Stories."

Irony always implies some repudiation, and in each of these works, irony is paramount. Almost always his stance is similar

to that of "This Majestic Lie," published the month of his
death, in which he describes his hero Johnnie as though he
were delivering his own eulogy:

*He attacked all obstacles in life in a spirit of contempt. . . . Somewhere
in him there was a sentimental tenderness, but it was like a light seen
afar at night; it came, went, appeared again in a new place, flickered,
flared, went out, left you in a void and angry. And if this sentimental
tenderness was a light, the darkness in which it puzzled you was his
irony of soul. This irony was directed first at himself; then at you; then
at the nation and the flag; then at God. It was a midnight in which you
searched for the elusive, ashamed spark of tender sentiment. [4:206]*

All-pervasive in his fiction, Crane's "irony of soul" seems to be
related to Lucretius's definition of irony as *"abdita vis quaedam,"*
a certain hidden force. So strong is this irony that it prompted
Berryman in his biography of Crane to quote Lucretius and to
write of Crane's work as a "riot of irony."[14] There may be
occasional sparks of pity flashing in the midnight of Crane's
irony, but there are none of hope. Crane's midnight is darker
than Matthew Arnold's; for Crane, to be true to one another is
impossible—we cannot even be true to ourselves. Life is a
continuous battle resulting in labor and sorrow: "I do not
confront it [life] blithely. I confront it with desperate resolution. . . . When I speak of a battle I do not mean want, and
those similar spectres. I mean myself and the inherent indo-
lence and cowardice which is the lot of all men."[15] To this
darkly and purely puritanical statement, Crane adds a touch of
Calvinism in a famous passage discussing his attempts to be
"as nearly honest as a weak mental machinery will allow"; he
ends by saying, "A man is sure to fail at it."[16] As if this were
not a dark enough picture to work within, Crane goes further
by ruling out hope: "Hope," he says, "is the most vacuous
emotion of mankind."[17]

The enormous repudiations which led Crane to nihilism may also lead to a logical extreme of intellectual if not physical catatonia, so that one could, like characters in Beckett's *Waiting for Godot* or Barth's *The End of the Road*, end by being paralyzed. Crane never succumbed to catatonia, but he went about as far in that direction as one could go and still function as a writer. In his craft, at least, he had a peculiar kind of luck: there were so many moribund dogmas to repudiate during the tag end of the last century—dogmas that seem patently absurd to us with twenty-twenty hindsight, but which few saw as such a century ago.

The Tradition

While Crane was battling the conventional and the traditional with one hand, with the other he held to tradition tenaciously and with such simple yet subtle methods that even the most exhaustive critical investigations have not entirely found him out. Yet it may have been tradition that saved Crane from literary catatonia. While he was shocking his literary friends with outrageous views, as well as outrageous writing, which seemed to fly in the face of all tradition, he periodically fled to the more settled conventionality of Port Jervis and Hartwood in rural New York. A few years later, he would flee the city in favor of a country estate in Sussex. In both places he seems to have taken some pleasure and comfort from playing traditional roles. In England, for example, he set himself up as a medieval squire in Brede place, a fourteenth-century manor house, complete with dogs under the dining room table and bulrushes in the halls. Crane was almost entirely classical in his lifestyle: he made forays into wars and cities, as Horace and Quintilian and Vida and others advise young poets to do, but he also followed their advice by living in the country. One must note the irony, however, in the fact that country living was supposed to provide the poet with the tranquility neces-

sary for contemplation; Crane was bothered by so many "Indians," as he called uninvited house guests and others, that he
had to hide in London for a time to do some writing.[18]

Traditional pastoral stability and a nostalgia for feudal life
may have provided a temporary counterbalance for sustaining
Crane's personal repudiations, but they could not also sustain
an art that embodied so many "new" movements that to
include literary impressionism, symbolism, determinism, existentialism, and nihilism barely scratches the surface. Without literary tradition—solid, enduring, ineradicable tradition—Crane's art would have been as anchorless as many say
it was. Parodying popular forms and minor genres, as Eric
Solomon suggests Crane did in many of his stories—the sentimental slum novel in *Maggie*, the traditional hunting yarn in
many of the *Sullivan County Tales and Sketches*, the dime novel
western in "The Bride Comes to Yellow Sky"—provided some
relief in Crane's early years, but it was never enough.[19] The
classical traditions, especially the traditions of the epic, are
always in the background of Crane's best fiction, and often in
the lesser works as well; occasionally they dominate.

Crane knew the classical tradition well enough for it to
influence his work significantly. Crane belongs to that select
company of writers with the intelligence, energy, will, and
patience to heed the heroic impulse which, as Roy Harvey
Pearce and James E. Miller, Jr., say, is part of the American
heritage in literature.[20] Thoreau had it, Whitman, Pound,
perhaps Stevens. Although cut off at twenty-eight, Crane
nevertheless walked the same path as these men, and even
more than they, in some ways, he worked within the tradition
established and made great by Milton, Virgil, and Homer.
Crane also knew those genres which exist both within and
apart from the epic and which were created by the Greeks:
tragedy and comedy. While most criticism of the epic follows
Aristotle's line of distinguishing among these three genres, it

should be remembered that Aristotle also granted that tragedy, for instance, had much in common with epic: "Anyone who knows about tragedy, good and bad, knows about epics, too, since tragedy has all the elements of epic poetry, though the elements of tragedy are not all present in the epic."[21]

That Stephen Crane knew the classics—knew them fairly well—should not be surprising. That it is mildly arresting testifies to how deeply ingrained is the notion of Crane as a pure example of the American literary dream calling for an entirely new literature utterly divorced from the past. It also attests to the variety and depth of Crane's newness, a quality that has been the preoccupation of Crane criticism for almost a century. Some contemporaries mention such epithets as "Greek" and "Homeric," but then as now the majority, including the most influential, dwell with the futurist H. G. Wells upon Crane's seemingly traditionless art: "It is as if the racial thought and tradition had been razed from his mind and its site ploughed and salted. . . . He is the first expression of the opening of a new period . . . beginning, as a growing mind must needs begin, with a record of impressions, a record of a vigor and intensity beyond all precedent."[22]

Disregarding the smattering of genuine critical evidence indicating that Crane had a nodding acquaintance with Homer and classical myth, little has been done to show that Crane's mind had not been ploughed and salted. And yet that evidence exists. Little has been uncovered in Crane's formal education to indicate a knowledge of the classics, but his private reading of the "classics of Greece and Rome" was extensive, even "voracious."[23] Crane could have acquired his attraction for classics from his good friend and classmate at Claverack College, Abram Lincoln Travis, who went on in later years to found the Travis Classical School in Syracuse. More likely, he got it from his heritage. Methodist ministers almost to a man, Crane's family on his mother's side was steeped in the classical tradition. In *The Classical Tradition*, Gilbert Highet gives a chapter to the nineteenth century, calling it "a century of scholarship." Twice as many books were written about ancient Greece and Rome in that century than in all the intervening ones combined. As educated people, the Pecks must have known that tradition well. Crane's maternal grandfather, Bishop George Peck, could read Greek and Hebrew, although he had never been to college.[24] And Stephen's Uncle Luther was a classical scholar.[25] Crane, then, came from an era and a family heritage in which the classics formed part of the fabric of daily life. Because he is acknowledged to have possessed a phenomenal memory, a genuinely significant intellect, and a voracious appetite for the "primitive," Crane could not have escaped learning about Homer, Virgil, and Ovid, any more than he could have avoided his great knowledge of the Bible. And even if, as Pratt has shown, he had not had a college course in Milton,[26] Crane in all likelihood would have been infused with the works of the English poet who most encompassed both the Bible and the classics.

Nevertheless, Crane cultivated the popular myth of the American writer as a "wild, shaggy barbarian,"[27] and as a part of that pose, he eschewed parading any real learning. As a result, his allusions to classical literature are few. Every now and then, however, they flash by in an invariably comic or ironic phrase. Playing the ignorant Westerner before a pompous Englishman, and having just returned from reporting the Greco-Turkish War, Crane said, "Say, when I planted those hoofs of mine on Greek soil I felt like the hull of Greek literature, like one gone over to the goldarned majority."[28] He punctured his century's plethora of classical scholarship again in an article about Hot Springs, Arkansas, in which he wrote that there baggagemen are "unintelligible" when they fight over customers "like a row of Homeric experts" (8:420). He even uses classical allusions to mock Christian missionary zeal in "Blood of the Martyr," where Christianity is used off-handedly to soften up the oriental populace for military conquest. The missionaries, says Prince Henry of Prussia, are to be fed on blood and "copies of Xenophon's 'Anabasis' " (8:735).

Occasionally, classical descriptions show up in Crane's unflattering portraits of women. In "Mr. Binks' Day Off," for example, Mrs. Binks "bristled with that brave anger which agitates a woman when she sees fit to assume that her husband is weak spirited. . . . Upon her face was a Roman determination. She was a personification of all manner of courages and rebellions and powers" (8:306). Conversely, Crane could describe women more flatteringly as "Junoesque" (8:708), in keeping with ideas about beauty in his day, or as resembling a "priestess in paintings of long-gone Mediterranean religions" (8:385). Like anyone else well schooled in the classics—until realism made personifications temporarily passé—Crane could personify abstract qualities as adroitly as had the ancients and the neoclassicists: "He wondered if incomprehensible justice were the sister of open wrong" (8:297); and a traffic jam in a narrow New York City street serves "to drive uncertain Reason from her tottering throne" (8:275).

Most strikingly significant is Crane's Homeric vision of life as a losing struggle for significance. In the Homeric world, only heroes could achieve so much as a brief flash in the encompassing darkness of the universe, and because there are no lasting heroes in Crane, the flashes there are even briefer than in the Greek epics. Like Homer's, Crane's work reveals an oppressive universe looming as an impassive background to the ultimately puny actions of even the best of men. For behind the gods and their machinations lay *Moira*, immutable fate, which even the gods could not control, and since Achilles and the lowliest slave share the same eventual end, there lay also the certainty that all human glory is fleeting. Such a view endured throughout the classical period. For every Roman emperor who proclaimed himself a god, a thousand tribunes rode in triumph through Rome accompanied by slave boys whispering in their ears that man is but dust.

To later classical ages, Homer's less than pious treatment of the gods was scandalous, and not until the decadence of post-Augustan Rome could poets like Petronius write with the same implied contempt as had Homer and as, much later, would Crane: "It was fear first created gods in the world."[29] Even so, that fear is somewhat real for both Homer and Crane, and if Greek heroes propitiate the gods through sacrifice and ritual, so too Crane's protagonists often react as though the gods, along with their attendant dragons, monsters, and demons, were real. The correspondent of "The Open Boat" complains to the "seven mad gods of the sea" in much the same way that Achilles complains to Thetis, and Henry Fleming flees before the "onslaught of redoubtable dragons." The list could fill a volume.

Ultimately, the picture in Crane is not much more naturalistic than it is in Homer or Virgil. Although such images of puny man before a universal backdrop become fewer after *The Red Badge* and as Crane matures, he is nevertheless reminded of them as late as 1897, when, in April, he is aboard the French steamer *Gaudiana* off Crete and witnessing the following scene: "A scouting torpedo boat as small as a gnat crawling on the enormous decorated wall [of Cretan cliffs] came from the obscurity of the shore. . . . Crete spread high and wide precisely like a painting from the absurd period when painters each tried to reproduce the universe on one canvas. . . . It was lonely and desolate like a Land of Despair if it were not for the venomous torpedo boat, which, after all, had been little more than a shadow on the water" (9:5–6). Crane never tried to "reproduce the universe" except ironically, and he was always aware that life may be important to us but not to the material universe.

"There must be something heroic" about the writer of epic, says Tillyard. He must be a rare writer who can temper "spontaneous genius" with an almost superhuman exercise of the will.[30] In spite of his youth, Stephen Crane was such a writer. Few question, and many have marveled at, the spontaneity of Crane's genius. For John Berryman, himself a composer of what James E. Miller calls the American "personal epic," Crane was much more formidable than mere spontaneity implies: "If Crane struck many of his contemporaries as a typically irresponsible 'genius,' his will strikes us—his patience and generalship and will," precisely the qualities Tillyard notes as common to all writers of great epic.

The next most impressive aspect of Crane's nature, again for Berryman, was "the heroic character of its effort." This character—along with intelligence, energy, and will—enabled Crane to gain the wisdom and experience usually considered prerequisites for attempting epic and usually demanding decades more to acquire. As a small boy, he passed over two grades in six weeks, and by the time he was fourteen he had an active vocabulary which included such words as "irascible," "memorial," and "pyrotechnic."[31] Before he had come of age, Crane had written a score of newspaper articles and sketches. He "learned about life" in the houses, bars, and opium dens of the Bowery; "at twenty-two he was living hand to mouth . . . at twenty-four he was the author of a classic . . . at twenty-five he was a star feature writer for a great syndicate in New York; and before he had reached his twenty-ninth birthday he was dead, leaving writing that filled twelve volumes in a collected edition."[32] And that is hardly half of it. He loved at least three or four women and not always serially;[33] defended a prostitute against the entire New York City Police Department; visited the South, the West, and

Mexico; was chased in deadly earnest across the Mexican desert by Ramon Colorado and his bandidos; endured a blizzard in Nebraska; was shipwrecked in January off the Florida coast; hunted deer, bear, and grouse in western New York; visited coal mines and prisons; lived in the ruins of an ancient manor house in England; socialized with Henry James, Theodore Roosevelt, and a host of other luminaries; became fast friends with Joseph Conrad, Harold Frederic, and others; and reported on both the Greco-Turkish and Spanish-American wars. With a vengeance and an energy almost unmatched in literary history, Crane obeyed the advice given by every composer of an *ars poetica* from Horace through the neoclassicists to the would-be writer of epic: *experience life.* To say that Crane was ill equipped as a writer of epic because he died too young is specious. If he was old at twenty, as Hamlin Garland said of him,[34] Crane must have been aged when he died eight years later.

In one major respect, Crane's newness is an old and necessary part of the epic tradition. As Bowra explains in *From Vergil to Milton*, Virgil repudiates Homeric notions of heroism by contrasting them with the Roman ideal of *pietas*, and Milton repudiates both Virgil and Homer by creating or expressing a heroism consisting neither of Homeric *areté* nor an earthbound pagan *pietas*, but rather of a "true patience and heroic martyrdom" that frees man from all considerations of time and space. Crane continues this tradition by repudiating all notions of heroism. Crane's fiction is undoubtedly "new," but it is a newness firmly rooted in an ancient tradition.

The epic is a genre whose history must be seen in terms of centuries rather than decades, but it is important to note that Wells's assessment of Crane as the initiator of a new period in literature may have been a remarkable insight. No significant war fiction since *The Red Badge* has been able to assert a traditional heroism. In fact, such fiction has reflected the two major themes of modern and postmodern American literature. First, there is the theme of undercutting traditional values, or at least mocking them. This theme is reflected in *A Farewell to Arms, The Naked and the Dead*, and certainly in *Catch-22*. But there is a second, and currently more exciting, theme: the search by postmodern writers, especially poets, for a new world view, or in Stevens's terms, a new supreme fiction. Such an heroic task seems paramount in the American long poem. Crane, then, is simultaneously traditional and modern or postmodern, for he uses the epic tradition to debase the notions of heroism contained in the classical tradition—a task which, if successful, repudiates former epics—and while working within that tradition attempts to search out a new vision of what it means to be heroic. Heroism is a mirror for cultural values; Crane attempted to construct a new supreme fiction out of the ruins of old heroic values.

The epic is the consummate genre, and heroism is its raison d'être. If its heroism is repudiated, the validity of the form is called in question. *The Red Badge* reveals in itself the enormity of Crane's repudiations, as well as the direction of his "newness."

Crane's knowledge and use of epic materials can be demonstrated in part by briefly examining the first chapter of *The Red Badge* as an updated imitation of the first book of the *Iliad*. Crane's novel, like the *Iliad*, begins *in medias res*, or more intimately, *in medio belli*, in the middle of the war, with the armies temporarily at rest. In both, there are rumors, an "assemblage," a quarrel, and a hero who retires from the assembly. There are flashbacks and forebodings, and a scene between the hero and his mother. When Mrs. Fleming gives Henry eight pairs of socks, this event seems more than coincidental. Had Achilles' mother better protected his feet, Achilles would have survived the Trojan War as Henry survived the Civil War.

Since the epic trappings and allusions of *The Red Badge* are imitative, it matters little that they have been incompletely examined. One passage in the first chapter, however, permits a glimpse into more significant aspects of the epic with which Crane was working. The concern of epic is in part to capture history for a people or a nation, and so to recreate the past. Recreating the past requires drawing prophetically from the future in order to reinforce the beliefs of these groups in themselves, in their destinies, and ultimately in their places in human or divine history. One common belief held in America and elsewhere—and held also by such groups as progressivists, millennialists, and various "peace societies" of the nineteenth century—was that as man evolved, he would become somehow "better." He would outgrow the brutish behavior of his forerunners and by doing so gradually slough off the ancient brutalities of war and hatred.[35] This view appears in the *North American Review* for November, 1817: "The world has gradually become better informed and more enlightened—other occupations beside the military have been introduced into society, and other views are generally entertained by judicious men."[36] Crane mocks this view, and perhaps these very words, in a strikingly similar passage from the first chapter of *The Red Badge*: "He had long despaired of witnessing a Greek-like struggle. Such would be no more, he had said. Men were better or more timid. Secular and religious education had effaced the throat-grappling instinct, or else firm finance held in check the passions" (2:5). One possibility to be conceded here is that Crane studied the literature of peace almost as thoroughly as Milton studied the devil. In any case, it is certain that Crane was here concerned with more than simply imitating Homer.

Traditional Repudiations

Crane's technique of denigrating myth in his best fiction had

an apprentice stage in his earlier and less well known work—
even at times in his early journalistic pieces. For example, in
the *New York Tribune* for February 21, 1892—about a year
before *Maggie* was first published—a piece appeared called
"The Last of the Mohicans."[37] In it, Crane manages to sketch
out rather lightly the same kind of pattern he was to follow
later: the simultaneous repudiation of illusion and of what
passes as art, which for Crane was often a perpetrator of
illusion. The sketch reports that the natives of Sullivan County, New York,

> *are continually shaking metaphorical fists at "The Last of the Mohi-*
> *cans" of J. Fenimore Cooper. . . . No consideration for the author, the*
> *literature or the readers can stay their hands, and they claim without*
> *reservation that the last of the Mohicans, the real and authentic last of*
> *the Mohicans, was a demoralized dilapidated inhabitant of Sullivan*
> *County.*
>
> *All know well that bronze god in a North American wilderness, that*
> *warrior with the eye of the eagle, the ear of the fox, the tread of a catlike*
> *panther, and the tongue of the wise serpent of fable.*

On the other hand, "The last of the Mohicans supported by
Sullivan County is a totally different character." This Indian

> *was no warrior who yearned after the blood of his enemies as the hart*
> *panteth for the water-brooks; on the contrary he developed a craving*
> *for the rum of the white man which rose superior to all other anx-*
> *ieties. . . . Arrayed in tattered, torn and ragged garments which some*
> *white man had thrown off, he wandered listlessly from village to*
> *village and from house to house, his only ambition being to beg, borrow*
> *or steal a drink. . . . He dragged through his wretched life in helpless*
> *misery.*

Myth-bursting attitudes are often peculiar to the young; at
twenty, Stephen Crane was tough-minded enough to attack

one of the deeply rooted myths of American consciousness. Mark Twain was fifty when he mocked Cooper, Crane much less than half that age. Furthermore, Crane's attack is more aggressive. "Fenimore Cooper's Literary Offences" strikes at Cooper's lack of verisimilitude, his lack of consistency, and his often shoddy prose. Crane, on the other hand, strikes square- ly at the heart of the matter. Both Twain and Crane were venting their distrust of romantic illusion, and both were attacking Cooper. While Twain is funnier, he stays mainly on the plane of literary offenses; Crane goes deeper, attacking not only literary offenses but the "noble savage" myth in its entire- ty. In Crane's treatment, Cooper falls very low. One ends by wondering whether or not Cooper could write well enough to send for seeds. In terms of its repudiations, Crane's concern is much more comprehensive than Twain's: by destroying the myth, Crane denigrates the artistic form generally considered to give expression to that myth—romance, a form earlier link- ed by Simms and later by Lutwack to the epic genre.[38]

But Crane cannot be called an advocate for some sort of natural white supremacy over the Red Indian. As he was willing, even eager, to do throughout his career, he turned the same technique, the same harsh attitude to the other side of the coin. In the same year, he published a sketch entitled "Not Much of a Hero," a story about "Tom Quick, the Indian Slayer, or the Avenger of the Delaware" (8:211–15). In it "a local writer" begins by trying to dramatize the life of this hero, but "after much study he was compelled to acknowledge that he could not make Quick's popular qualities run in a noble and virtuous groove." This angered some young men who "going westward to massacre the devoted red man with a fell purpose and a small calibre revolver always carry a cheap edition of Tom Quick's alleged biography." Quick, it turns out, is any- thing but a traditional American hero; he even murders Indi- ans in their sleep. The sketch ends with the following possibilities: "The deeds which are accredited to him may be fictional ones and he may have been one of those sturdy and bronzed woodsmen who cleared the path of civilization. Or the accounts may be true and he was a monomaniac upon the subject of Indians as suggested by the dramatist. Or the accounts may be true and he a man whose hands were stained with unoffending blood, purely and simply a murderer." In any case, Crane seems more than willing to accept the realistic accounts from the oral traditions as true, or at least truer.

Crane was to go on in this antimythical vein throughout his career, but for the most part, it was only when he attacked the older, more classical myths and genres that his art reached toward greatness. It would usually be at its best only when the elements of epic, or of tragedy or comedy, were added to the mythical and employed to repudiate the underlying assumptions of myth and genres, assumptions based almost entirely on the notion that man is significant in the universe and capable of achieving a given heroic ideal.

In *Maggie*, Crane mocks the American ideal that a woman need only remain pure and endure long enough for things to turn out well, for her to reach some longed-for "higher" realm. As Solomon suggests, he uses the sentimental slum novel to give *Maggie* part of its form and parodic quality, but Crane's irony is powerful and cannot be contained by ephemeral genres, and so he goes much further and deeper into literary tradition to expose this illusion: he presents a domestic classical tragedy of the slums. He inverts and unites tragedy and a feminine version of the Horatio Alger fable;[39] the result is an inversion of the Persephone myth. In the myth, the heroine ends by dividing her time between the throne of Hades and a garden-fresh springtime world. Maggie, conversely, moves from one hell to another. One hell is no less or more endurable than another, but for Maggie, there is no springtime world, no garden, no warm, life-stirring sun. There is only death, only

Hades, each a cold and lifeless stream at midnight.

In *The Red Badge of Courage*, Crane most fully lashes out against the epic and against epic expressions of heroism. He depicts all former epic concepts of heroism—Homeric *areté*, in which individual excellence is all; Virgilian *pietas*, which demands that the hero sacrifice all to the gods, family, country, and "destiny"; and Miltonic "true patience and heroic martyrdom"—and abolishes them. In the end there is no heroism and so no epic, just as at the end of *Maggie* no order is restored out of chaos, no justice is revived, and no tragedy occurs.

Crane's western trip in 1895 resulted in a number of western tales, most notably "The Blue Hotel" and "The Bride Comes to Yellow Sky." These are the comic and tragic sides to the death of the heroic age in the American West, and both employ elements of the epic to universalize the significance of that death. For when the heroic age failed in Yellow Sky and died in Fort Romper, there ended, again, the dream of the West that began in literature when Odysseus sailed out between the Pillars of Hercules in search of the Isles of the Blessed. These stories recreate a transitional moment in the history of the world that occurs over and over again: of Rome incorporating, but nevertheless destroying, Greece; of white men replacing the heroic civilizations of the American Indian and frontiersman with a more domestic society; of the industrial East defeating the West (which is to say McKinley defeating Bryan or Hamilton finally winning over Jefferson). It is the old story of the group defeating the individual.

"The Blue Hotel" especially expresses the nameless quality in man that allows him to conspire against the individual in the name of "safety" or "progress" for the group, the town, the nation, the species. This is as old and terrifying a story as *Antigone* and at least as new as Nazi Germany. "The Blue Hotel" explores the flaw in man that allows him to act in a group as he would never act alone. The group strips away all traces of value in an individual and then defines him as an animal, all without the group member's having to face the guilt. Guilt may be lost in collective rationalizations. "We're all in it," says the Easterner, to make himself feel better; but self-absolution comes from the cowboy, ignorant and blind, who remarks, "Well, I didn't do anything, did I?" (5:170).

The Monster would have been defined or catalogued by Aristotle as one of the four types of epic: ethical. In fact, it is what someone called an "epic of democracy," in which an honest, ethical, and upright man discovers that the group cannot be defeated by one who would live within it. "The Monster" is not Henry Johnson; rather it is the group whose fear drives it into amorality.

"The Open Boat" grew out of Crane's shipwreck experience off Datona Beach, Florida, in early January of 1897. It is a very modern story, an epic reduced to what Aristotle calls the epic's "universal form," an epic without episodes. If *Paradise Regained* is Milton's personal sequel to *Paradise Lost*, "The Open Boat" is Crane's personal sequel to *The Red Badge*, and it most fully fits the requirements for the American "personal epic."[40] It is in this story that Crane effectively repudiates his former work. "When it occurs to a man that nature does not regard him as important, and that she feels she would not maim the universe by disposing of him, he at first wishes to throw bricks at the temple" (5:84–85). This passage may describe Crane's work up to "The Open Boat," but there is a final clause that implies a significant change: "and he hates deeply the fact that there are no bricks and no temples." If in his last works Crane disdains the epic, it is perhaps because he no longer sees the epic as a temple to be brought down, nor, possibly, does he then consider his works to be bricks: "Script," he once wrote to Nellie Crouse, "is an infernally bad vehicle for thoughts. I know that, at least."[41] As a result, the epic looms large for the last time in "The Open Boat." The archetypal journey of the four men in an open boat has epic proportions and epic significance but no epic outcome.

Crane's work progresses from the rather simple "pro-toepics" of the early sketches and reports (to be discussed later) to the rejection of Christian and classical myths about a higher world in *Maggie* to the extremely well wrought and encompassing denial of knowledge of any kind in "The Open Boat." One is tempted to say that Crane progresses from iconoclastic satirist to confirmed nihilist, but that would be misleading. Crane was always a nihilist. There is nothing to hold on to at the end of his most important works; the difference is generally one of quality or perhaps clarity of expression. The nihilism of *Maggie* is angry, muddled, overly insistent when compared with "The Open Boat," whose nihilism is ice-clear, pristine, cold, hard, beautiful.

The progression also involves both scope and focus. In *Maggie*, Crane denies the existence of "heaven," or anything beyond the hell of the materialistic universe. In *The Red Badge*, he disavows many sacred beliefs: heroism that can last, meaning in war, the validity of memory and history. In "The Bride" and "The Blue Hotel," heroism is short-lived to the point of existing only in a momentary flash of action, and even then it must be retrieved from the past by Scratchy Wilson or from an idea by the Swede. The scope of these stories is as broad as that of *Maggie* and only a little more terrestrial. "The Bride" denies the long dream of an unexplored "Wild West" where men may be free from the restrictions of collective life. "The Blue Hotel" demonstrates that a modern, group-dominated society of the kind that populates Whilomville and Fort Romper will not allow the idea of the West to continue or even to exist except behind visions of a hero-colored past. The scope of this story includes the implication that mankind will henceforth be dominated by the mob—a prophecy becoming fact. Crane finally reaches a culmination of his repudiation of epic in "The

Open Boat." In this story, the idea that man can know anything, anything at all, about heaven, hell, earth, or self is denied, flatly denied. Even the imagination seems to be denied, and without the imagination, there can be no art. After that, he lapsed in the *Whilomville Stories*, most of which reflect a *Bucolics* attitude, a kind of "utopia," as Levenson says. Then, too, there came the Greek stories—*Active Service*, a parody of modern love and lovers, and also "Death and the Child," a story of denial more emphatic than "The Open Boat" because less ambiguous.

Protoepics of Consciousness

Among the many qualities that make the epic great is the fact of its reputation as the supreme literary genre of human consciousness.[42] More than any other form, it attempts to encompass the whole of human experience from the womb to the grave and from the chaotic beginnings of the world to the abyss of its end. The psychology of epic is one of an individual hero struggling to escape from the cave—an archetype of undifferentiated unconsciousness and, beginning with Virgil, violence. The hero escapes from the cave into consciousness by attempting and struggling to perceive reality on its own terms. Unfortunately, consciousness creates the pain of alienation from the rest of the material universe. But the struggle is necessary for epic—indeed, it may define epic—because the condition is both universal and individual—everyone faces it and yet must face it alone—and because it requires an epic strength of purpose and control. The final test of consciousness is the ability to face that alienation in many forms, not the least of which is the fact of mortality. If the first two stages of what may be called, somewhat redundantly, the epic of consciousness are the cave and heightened consciousness or alienation, the final stage is transcendence. Transcendence is created by fusing the unconscious and the conscious into unconscious consciousness, a state akin to the mystical in which the hero transcends both himself and the "other" of the material universe by coming to *know* objective reality without relinquishing consciousness, something accomplished factually less easily than syntactically.

According to Jung, the archetypes of the undifferentiated unconscious, as well as the transcendent conscious-unconsciousness, may involve metaphors of actual or potential enclosure: the sea, fountains, pools, forests, caves, houses, or cities.[43] Hence epics often begin with settings or descriptions of enclosures, and as the heroes struggle toward consciousness, these enclosures may appear again and again. Achilles retires to his shelter in the first book of the *Iliad*; the *Odyssey* opens with the hero peering out from Calypso's cave; the *Aeneid* begins with an Olympic discussion of Carthage and Troy, in that epical time the two great cities of the Mediterranean, both doomed;[44] Dante's *Hell*, itself a cave of enclosed violence, opens with the hero wandering aimlessly through a dark wood;[45] and Milton's Satan begins in Hell.

Dante, Aeneas, and Odysseus explore many caves throughout their wanderings, and each finds a kind of transcendence. Odysseus, after reestablishing his kingdom, finds that he is to be the eternal wanderer, the man who always has one more journey to make. Aeneas, in the midst of Hades, hears prophecies of the greatness of Rome, and he knows their realization will give meaning to *lacrimae rerum* and to his struggling and death. When Dante finally approaches the transcendence of heaven, he is so overwhelmed that the experience transcends words. Each hero escapes the cave, faces alienation, and transcends both.

Archetypes of the unconscious appear regularly in Crane's work from first to last. In some they are vehicles for expressing misperceived reality only. In others, particularly the better works, the entire prototype for the epic is present: journeying into the dark places of the mind; facing death or the threat of death occasionally, but always experiencing alienation; escaping.[46] It is important to note that rarely, if ever, is the escape permanent in the best works, and that the third requisite—transcendence—is perhaps never effected in Crane, although the accouterments for transcendence occasionally appear. That is, the protagonists are placed in situations where transcendence ought to be possible, but they either fail to recognize the possibility or fail to act upon it.

Instead, chaos dominates Crane's earliest fiction; its enclosures, somewhat like Plato's famous cave, are places where perception is at best secondhand. In Crane's first work, "Uncle Jake and the Bell Handle" (8:3–7), a farmer and his niece journey to the city to sell his surplus produce. Their entrance into the city is described in terms of enclosure and chaos: "Soon the houses began to appear closer together, there were more tin cans and other relics strewn about the road-side, they began to get views of multitudes of back-yards, with washes on lines; grimy, smoky factories; stock yards filled with discordant mobs of beasts; whole trains of freight cars, standing on tracks; dirty children, homeless dogs and wandering pigs. Beer saloons commenced to loom up occasionally" (8:4).

Uncle Jake is so overwhelmed by the chaos that that atmosphere is soon reproduced in his imagination. When he tugs an unattached bell handle, a waiter simultaneously (but independently) bangs a dinner gong. Utterly misperceiving events, Jake is convinced that he has become "a critir hounded by the dogs of the law" for calling out "the police force or the ambulance corps" (8:6) and for plunging the country into civil war. Jake and his niece escape by racing for home through an alien labyrinth of city streets which "if it could be mapped would look like a brain-twisting Chinese puzzle."

Although amazingly precocious for thirteen-year-old Crane, the story is slight. Nevertheless, it shows that already

Crane is concerned with labyrinths of mind and consciousness; already he is testing his characters by sending them into places of enclosed violence and labyrinthian complexity where they fail to transcend situations of alienation because they misperceive reality.

The first nearly complete prototypical epic of consciousness in the Crane canon is perhaps the 1893 story "The Reluctant Voyagers" (8:14–33). Here two characters enter a frightening, violent world of the sea, and in facing death become somewhat aware of themselves as differentiated from the "other." They are rescued into a potentially transcendent situation, but because they fail to transcend themselves and that other, they fail in a primary epic task: to perceive reality correctly and to deal with that perception transcendingly.

Two men—a "freckled man" and a "tall man"—rent bathing suits. The freckled man is given a suit many times too large by a bathhouse attendant whose misperception foreshadows the later misperceptions of the two swimmers. Throughout his works, by placing some distorting force or object between the viewer and the object viewed, Crane signified his belief that man could seldom correctly perceive reality:[47] "A bath-clerk was looking at the world with superior eyes through a hole in a board" (8:15). To avoid the embarrassment of being seen wearing such an oversized suit, the freckled man, with the tall man following, swims far out into the water. Here he sees an abandoned raft and swims to it. Lounging on the raft, the two men lose track of time, discovering too late that they have drifted far from shore. They spend the night on the Atlantic. Now the frightening passions of the unconscious mind, symbolized by the ocean at night, begin to take over: "As night settled over the sea, red and green lights began to dot the blackness. There were mysterious shadows between the waves. . . . The voyagers cringed at magnified foam on distant crests. A moon came and looked at them. 'Somebody's here,' whispered the freckled man" (8:20). Faced with a threat of death and differentiated starkly from the "other" of the sea, they become afraid and their fears are magnified. The inevitable consequence of consciousness—alienation—is made explicit by the appearance of "a moon"—not *the* moon, the known and comforting moon, but *a* moon.

They are finally rescued by a passing ship. Given food and beds and eventually set ashore, the two men show themselves to be utterly unredeemed when they berate the captain for providing them with plain fare, ordinary beds, and a landing site far from their embarkation point. Further, in the process of being set ashore, they are so overwrought that the skiff overturns and the oarsman is nearly drowned. Not the events, but the description of those events is protoepical.

Entering the archetypal sea, the two become frightened by alienation and possible death. When rescued they are placed in another enclosure. Had they learned from their encounter with the unconscious, this would have a potential for transcendence reminiscent of Dante's return from Hell. After traversing the eight circles, Dante emerges at the end of the *Inferno* marveling at a heaven of stars. So too the reluctant voyagers:

They followed him [the captain] along the deck, and fell down a square, black hole in the cabin. It was a little den, with walls of vanished whiteness. A lamp shed an orange light. In a sort of recess two little beds were hiding. A wooden table, immovable, as if the craft had been builded around it, sat in the middle of the floor. Overhead the square hold was studded with a dozen stars. A footworn ladder led to the heavens. [8:4]

As in many of Crane's other stories, pride keeps the two men from recognizing their own salvation. The reader, on the other hand, is given a glimpse of a transcending reality. In "The

Reluctant Voyagers," that reality is classical, not Christian. The ship, for instance, is bound for Athens, New York; the rented swimsuit is "a regular toga"; and the captain is extraordinary in a decidedly classical way. In fact, he is a kind of *deus ex machina* common to epic and not uncommon to Crane, since Gibson has shown that the Cheery Man of *The Red Badge* is also this kind of character.[48] The captain helps the two reluctant voyagers as much as Athena helps Odysseus, similarly floating on a raft, to reach land: "The captain produced ponderous crackers and some broiled ham. Then he vanished in the firmament like a fantastic comet" (8:25). At other times his legs appear "among the stars," he brings coffee "from the sky," and he also disappears "from the sky." Later, when the tall man berates him for his supposedly shoddy treatment of the voyagers, "the captain howled and vanished in the sky."

The *deus ex machina*, roundly damned in an age of realism, and certainly peculiar to find in the work of a man whose antecedents supposedly do not predate the nineteenth century, is a device for helping heroes do what they cannot do alone. In formal epic, the hero almost always recognizes the divinity, if only after the fact of the contact, and gives thanks. In modern fiction the *deus ex machina*, owing partly to the demands of realism, is usually well disguised, and may in part be following Aristotle's dictum that poets should prefer the "probable impossibility to the impossible probability." In "The Reluctant Voyagers," the protagonists not only fail to recognize the divine aid, but actually and actively berate the giver, assuming in their pride that they have some inalienable right to salvation of a very high social and material quality. The story employs this classical device to strengthen the reader's perception of the protagonists' misperceptions. Crane's realism remains intact for the most part, but the use, however obliquely, of this simple and ancient device in "The Reluctant

Voyagers" gives classical form and timbre to this simple tale, which some misread as not only conventional but hardly competent.[49]

Between "Uncle Jake and the Bell Handle" (1885) and "The Reluctant Voyagers" (1893) comes a host of stories, tales, and sketches, the most remarkable of which, as a group, are perhaps "The Sullivan County Sketches." If "Uncle Jake" fulfills the first criterion of the epic of consciousness and "The Reluctant Voyagers" includes all three, several of the "Sullivan County Sketches" include the first two: the "cave" of unconsciousness and violence along with alienation and the facing of either potential or actual death. Of course, the wilderness pervades this collection of sketches about rural New York but in some, such as "Four Men in a Cave," the cave dominates. Berryman's Freudian delight, the story depicts four men exploring a cave and falling into a room-sized vault. In the middle of the vault is a drunken man who stands before a table demanding that the "little man" play cards with him. The little man plays, loses, and then all four men are told to get out. They do. It is a slight and funny story on the surface, but once again the description leads towards something else. The man's voice "was a true voice from a cave, cold, solemn and damp" (8:228), and he speaks in "sepulchral tones." A damp classical hell, not a burning Christian one, this cave includes an "altar-like stone," the deck of cards looks like "a little volume," and facing these hapless Actaeons are two "cadaverous hounds, licking their red lips" (8:229).

One need not psychoanalyze this story, written a couple of years before Freud started full-time dream interpretation, to believe that Stephen Crane, whose Methodist minister father wrote books and tracts warning young people against drinking and gambling, is here exploring the dark places of his own mind. There is no inclusion of even a potential transcendence (the men's deliverance is signaled by a curt "Go"), but there is an exploration of the cave and the threat of death (the drunken man pulls a knife on them). The story goes further than "Uncle Jake," but not so far as "The Reluctant Voyagers." Yet, in spite of the humor, "Four Men in a Cave" serves to demonstrate how unflinchingly Crane could penetrate his own psyche, for exploring the cave is tantamount to the individual's exploring his own mind—particularly that part filled with those irrational and unconscious fears which are often objectified by dragons, monsters, and demons.[50] Placed in a chronological sequence, the three stories also indicate a developing trend in Crane's work, a trend toward working out an epic sequence in which all the elements are included except that of actual transcendence.

Many other "Sullivan County Sketches" fall somewhere within the spectrum of the three steps of the epic of consciousness. "Bear and Panther" (8:238–39) provides an ironical glimpse at man before alienation, at man barely separated from the cave. Here two men are watching the entrance to a cave, the den of a panther. While they provide themselves with cover, they seem to do so not out of fear but merely to afford themselves an unhurried shot when the panther comes out. Instead of a full-grown panther emerging, a bear pops out carrying a panther kitten in its mouth. After killing this kitten and another, the bear loses a fight with the mother of the kittens. "The hunters then shot the panther."

Hardly two pages long, this story shows man undifferentiated from the natural world outside himself. This lack of differentiation is different from the transcendent union of man and nature sought as the epic goal. Rather, it demonstrates the bestiality and violence of the cave before alienation and transcendence. This condition is pre-historical and as such is pre-epical.

In "A Ghoul's Accountant" (8:240–42) Crane returns to his familiar theme of alienation from the cave. Here the little man in the wilderness is forced out of his sleeping bag and into the dark woods at night to a cabin where the "ghoul" and another man are haggling over the cost of thirty-three bushels of potatoes at sixty-four and a half cents per bushel. They demand that the little man compute the total for them. He does so and thus passes what seems to be some sort of archetypal test. His reward, however, or his "transcending" deliverance, is to be summarily kicked out the door and back into the night. Fear, alienation, and a touch of the primitively mystical, but no transcendence.

In "The Octopush" everything comes together—the unconscious (a wilderness, a pond, tombs, graves, and caves) and the differentiating element of alienation—except for the experience of transcendence. The story begins "once upon a time" (8:230) with four men who go "into the wilderness" to fish in one of those ponds peculiar to the East, which, because recently created by damming a woodland stream after the surrounding land has been timbered, is dotted by the "squat stumps" of trees "in multitudes." A self-appointed guide with "a voice from the tomb" places each man on one of the stumps, thus physically isolating each from the others. He then proceeds to find a stump of his own and watch the day go by. At some point he begins drinking and by sundown is roaring drunk. About dusk the four men ask to be picked up in the guide's boat, but the guide drunkenly refuses: "Suddenly it struck each that he was alone, separated from humanity by impassable gulfs. All those things which come forth at night began to make noises. Unseen animals scrambled and flopped among the weeds and sticks. Weird features masqueraded awfully in robes of shadow. Each man felt that he was compelled to sit on something that was damply alive" (8:232). As alienation increases, "a ghost-like mist came and hung upon the waters. The pond became a grave-yard. The grey tree-trunks and dark logs turned to monuments and crypts" (8:233).

In "Uncle Jake and the Bell Handle," Jake saves himself from nothing but what his own imagination has conjured. In "The Reluctant Voyagers," a divine presence rescues the protagonists from a comic but real danger, but the two men simply fail to recognize it. The rescue in "The Octopush" lies somewhere in between. The four men are rescued by someone else, but not from a real danger, merely from a genuine discomfort and embarrassment. And their rescuer is neither divine nor fortuitous since the guide himself is responsible for placing the fishermen in the situation. He can hardly be called divine since he rescues the men only to rescue himself from the illusions of his own besotted imagination. He is afraid and now seeks the company and safety of other men. Nothing epical here, only the protoepical elements of the cave and alienation of consciousness. Nothing classical either, except perhaps for what Berryman calls Crane's pervasive irony.

One short sketch, "Killing His Bear" (8:249–51), out of all the "Sullivan County Sketches" seems to fulfill the epic prototype. Here the little man is hunting in the wilderness shortly after sunset and becomes mildly frightened by the "armies of shadows" produced by the failing light. But when he hears the dog on the trail of a bear, his imagination takes over: "Swift pictures of himself in a thousand attitudes under a thousand combinations of circumstances, killing a thousand bears, passed panoramically through him." Exactly as in *The Red Badge*, the hero is not only frightened by his imagination, but that imagination also attempts to make a virtue out of alienation by having him do unheard-of deeds in his mind. Soon, by a stroke of luck, the bear heads towards him and he shoots. The result is described in terms of a genuine, if temporary, transcendence: "The earth faded to nothing. Only space and the game, the aim and the hunter. Mad emotions, powerful enough to rock worlds, hurled through the little man, but did not shake his tiniest nerve." This transcendence, however, is either illusory or temporary, at least for the reader, because of the irony of the description of the man's reaction to the bear's death: "The little man yelled and sprang forward, waving his hat as if he were leading the cheering of thousands. He ran up and kicked the ribs of the bear. Upon his face was the smile of a successful lover." Transcendence is at best temporary in Crane, largely because, as Holton notes, "clear seeing can also be learned or forgotten, can be acquired or lost."[51]

Before writing *The Red Badge*, in which formal epic comes to the fore, Crane experimented with protoepic and was learning as he went along. Transcendence did not come then, but he knew it belonged to the process. He must have known it, not only because he presents it in potentiality in "The Reluctant Voyagers," but also because a stark outline for the protoepic, as well as for his version of the formal epic, appears in Crane's revised version of "In the Depths of a Coal Mine," in a paragraph describing his descent down a shaft of Dunmore mine Number Five in Scranton:[52]

The dead black walls slid swiftly by. They were a swirling dark chaos on which the mind tried vainly to locate some coherent thing, some intelligible spot. One could hold fast to the iron bars and listen to the roar of this implacable descent. When the faculty of balance is lost, the mind becomes a confusion. The will fought a great battle to comprehend something during this fall, but one might as well have been stumbling among the stars. The only thing was to await revelation. [8:593–94].

While Crane had rejected Christianity when he was very young, he nevertheless seems even in these early sketches to have been trying to work out a religious or mythical or possibly even mystical solution to the problem of transcendence. The caves of these sketches are classical in their damp gloominess, as most caves are in reality. And the one transcendent figure in them is classical rather than Christian in his metaphorical movements between earth and stars. Crane's descent into the cave at Dunmore mine Number Five was the journey of a classicist who went to battle unconsciousness. But he also sought a transcendence beyond the unconscious, a transcendence of an unconscious consciousness which might be found by "tumbling among the stars." Crane was a classicist who fought for consciousness and waited for revelation.

The American antithesis of classicism is transcendentalism. And Crane believed in things antithetical to transcendentalism. He did not believe that there was some ordering force in the universe, but rather that outside of man lay only chaos. If the transcending power existed, it did not exist "out there." Normally, this notion is considered as a twentieth-century phenomenon, but its roots lay philosophically with the Greeks and scientifically and psychologically in the nineteenth century, and even then it was hardly confined to esoteric research. William James, for example, as early as 1881, was already popularizing the "reflex theory of the mind, a philopsychological counterpart to impressionism." This theory explains that the events occurring in the universe are chaotic, and that only some organizing faculty of the mind gives us the impression that things are ordered:

Is not the sum of your actual experience taken at this moment and impartially added together an utter chaos? . . . Is it not the only condition of your mental sanity in the midst of them [experiences] that most of them should become nonexistent for you, and that a few others . . . should evoke from places in your memory that have nothing to do with this scene associates to combine with them in what we call a rational train of thought—rational, because it leads to a conclusion

which we have some organ to appreciate? We have no organ or faculty
to appreciate the simply given order. The real world as it is given
objectively at this moment is the sum total of all its being and events
now. But can we think of such a sum? Can we realize for an instant
what a cross-section of all existence at a definite point of time would be?
[No.] . . . Yet just such a collateral contemporaneity, and nothing else,
is the real order of the world. It is an order with which we have nothing
to do but get away from it as soon as possible. As I said, we break it: we
break it into histories, and we break it into arts, and we break it into
sciences; and then we begin to feel at home.

For Crane, as for both Jameses, if transcendence lay anywhere, it lay in man himself. For Henry James the answer lay
in seizing upon the imagination and creating out of it the most
intricate order possible. Certainly, he tried to get close to what
Stevens later called "not Ideas about the thing, but the Thing
Itself" (i.e., reality), but he did so by trying to recreate the
"Thing" in the imagination. The problem for Crane lay in an
entirely different direction: the ordering faculty, the imagination—and its "breakings" into histories, arts, and sciences—is
a lie. The descendent of more than two centuries of puritans
on this continent, Crane was one of the last puritans. He had
to try to see the truth, see it "raw," as he said, without the
intervention of ordering faculties like memory or imagination.

To penetrate memory, imagination, and related faculties
which order the chaotic events occurring in the universe and
by doing so to confront reality is Crane's epic task. Crane may
join company with Whitman and Melville and a few others as
precursors of Wallace Stevens's search for a supreme fiction to
replace the world view of Milton's epic. The jar set in Tennes-
see is celebrated by Stevens for its power to organize the
wilderness. But Stevens's jar is remarkably similar in its power
to the stone table organizing the scene in "Four Men in a
Cave"; the wooden table of "The Reluctant Voyagers," which

seems to be "immovable, as if the craft had been builded around it"; the stove in Alex Williams's home in *The Monster*; and the stove in the middle of a room of the Palace Hotel in "The Blue Hotel," a stove set against the chaos of the storm outside. All of these objects organize chaos, but while they might provide the first efforts for creating a supreme fiction for Stevens, for Crane they present false pictures in the very fact of their organizing power.

Stevens's revelation that the imagination, once decreated, could build a more realistic transcendence, a new supreme fiction, was preceded by Stephen Crane, who spent his career decreating the imagination. This included a decreation of art, and his decreation of art included a decreation of the most revered genre in literature: the epic. That decreation and a failed attempt to find a supreme fiction to replace the old epic views surround the story of *The Red Badge of Courage*.

*The immense poetry of war and the poetry of
a work of the imagination are two different
things. In the presence of the violent reality
of war, consciousness takes the place of the
imagination. . . . It follows that the poetry of
war . . . constitutes a participating in the heroic.*

WALLACE STEVENS[1]

*War is a teacher who educates through violence;
and he makes men's characters fit their conditions.*

THUCYDIDES

Chapter Two

The Anger of Henry Fleming: The Epic of Consciousness & *The Red Badge of Courage*

The Red Badge of Courage establishes Stephen Crane as a writer formally and solidly within the great tradition established and fostered by Homer, Virgil, Milton, and others. While including many of the trappings and conventions and much machinery of formal epic, *The Red Badge* also shares with the epic a more essential quality: the tradition of epic competition. Although greatly oversimplified, a broad review of that tradition would read rather like a social history of Western society over the last twenty-five hundred years.

Because it began traditionally with Homer and historically sometime before 400 B.C. in the eastern Mediterranean, the tradition of epic competition is as old as any in Western literature. One version of an ancient romantic work called "The Contest of Homer and Hesiod," for example, relates how Homer and Hesiod competed to determine who was the best poet.[2] A comparison of the recitations, as well as the judgment of the audience, indicates that Homer was clearly the better of the two. Yet the king of Chalcis in Euboea, where the contest was reportedly held, awarded the prize to Hesiod, saying that "he who called upon men to follow peace and husbandry should have the prize rather than one who dwelt upon war and slaughter."

While demonstrating the antiquity of epic competition, the story makes another point vital to the tradition and to *The Red Badge*: epics and epic poets do not always compete over literary values. Although the reputations of Virgil and Milton as epic poets rest in part upon how well they compare aesthetically with Homer, nonliterary factors such as cultural and religious values also claim the attention of these men. The most important of these values for the epic is the different ideal of heroism held by each poet, particularly regarding the object of man's duty. The Homeric epics may be termed "individual" because they tend to glorify the individual man. Virgil's is a "group" epic because it glorifies Rome and defines the state as a more worthy object of duty than the individual. Milton attempts, among other things, to glorify a Puritan God and to justify worthiness in his sight as the object of man's duty. To the degree that Milton saw man's task as an attempt to reproduce God's kingdom in the self and community of Christians, *Paradise Lost* and *Paradise Regained* become "group" epics. One way, then, to look at the history of the West is as a movement from man being accountable only for himself—man as individualistic and ego-centric—to man as part of something larger, more enduring and significant than himself.

Each of these views finds an embodiment in a great epic poet's notion of heroism, for heroism consists of fulfilling the demands of duty. The Homeric hero ascribes to the code of *areté*, which demands that he strive ceaselessly for the first prize. The driving force behind all the hero's actions, *areté* often connotes values different from Roman and Christian virtue. Virtues lauded over the last fifteen hundred years and more—loyalty, honesty, charity, fair play—are simply not part of the code of *areté*; Achilles deserted the field and his friends and spent much of the war in an adolescent funk and Odysseus was a liar and a cheat, but both were great warriors and so have the highest *areté*.[3]

What distinguishes Virgil's Aeneas from Homeric heroes is not the greatness of his deeds but the reasons for performing them. Virgil's epithet for Aeneas is "pius," a term denoting more than "pious" for Aeneas is also "dutiful." Careful to pour appropriate libations for the gods, Aeneas also is concerned for his family and his destiny. Seeker of peace, invincible in war, believer in law, Aeneas is the heroic ideal of the *Romanum Imperium* of Augustus.

To explain how Aeneas, a second-level Homeric hero in the *Iliad*, became a metaphor for Rome in the *Aeneid* would require several volumes of social, intellectual, and literary history that would carry one from Attic to Roman civilizations. The problem for Virgil, however, was that Homer still dominated the genre in Augustan Rome and his heroes were still revered. As a result, Virgil was forced to compete unevenly with Homer. If Rome were superior to Homeric Greece, then the great Roman epic would have to be superior to the Homeric epics. Virgil succeeded, at least politically, by elevating the Roman hero and debasing the Homeric, elevating *pietas* and debasing *areté*. Thus Turnus, *alius Achilles*, embodies *areté*, and when Aeneas kills him in the poem's final lines, Virgil metaphorically "kills" Achilles, *areté*, and the Homeric epic. Later Christian epic poets such as Tasso, Camoens, Dante, and Ariosto also despise *areté*—which they saw as almost identical to *hubris*—and show their contempt by assigning it as a quality belonging to their heroes' enemies. Milton's Satan belongs to this type, and in spite of his attractiveness as a Homeric or Shelleyan hero, he is nevertheless a personification of evil.[4] Milton's concept of heroism and duty is as complex as his use of the epic medium, but it is also clear that genuine heroism lies in "true patience and heroic martyrdom." The real Christian hero seeks glory by following the New Testament and dedicates his deeds *ad majoram gloriam Dei*. How one plays the game determines whether one wins or loses.

When Crane includes these notions of heroism and duty in *The Red Badge*, he undertakes a task crucial to writing epics. Because these concepts of heroism and duty are among the most influential in Western history, when Crane denigrates and replaces them, he rewrites, in a very real sense, the cultural history of the West.

Inward Repudiations

The first chapter of *The Red Badge* presents heroic ideals in the mind of Henry Fleming, a "youth" inclined by instinct toward *areté*, but checked by "religious and secular education" so that he feels himself to be a part of something much larger than himself. Henry is introduced into the story and is immediately engaged in a debate with himself over "some new thoughts that had lately come to him" (2:4). On the one hand, he sees himself in expressly Homeric terms, with "peoples secure in the shadow of his eagle-eyed prowess" (2:5). In retrospect, he remembers having "burned several times to enlist. Tales of great movements shook the land. They might not be distinctly Homeric, but there seemed to be much glory in them. He had read of marches, sieges, conflicts, and he had longed to see it all. His busy mind had drawn for him large pictures extravagant in color, lurid with breathless deeds" (2:5). On the other hand, his mother, the voice of Christian-group ideals, "had discouraged him." Her advice upon his enlistment is the advice of the group: "Don't go a-thinkin' you can lick the hull rebel army at the start, because yeh can't. Yer just one little feller amongst a hull lot of others, and yeh've got to keep quiet an' do what they tell yeh" (2:7). Contrary to Henry's Grecian mood—he would rather have heard "about returning with his shield or on it"—his mother's relationship to Christianity is everywhere apparent. Her only remark upon hearing of Henry's enlistment is "The Lord's will be done," and when he leaves she says simply, "The Lord'll take keer of us all" (2:7).

As a surrogate mother, the army too puts a damper on his heated individualism. Before leaving home, "he had felt growing within him the strength to do mighty deeds of arms," but after spending "months of monotonous life in a camp," Henry comes "to regard himself as part of a vast blue demonstration" (2:8).

Throughout the first half of *The Red Badge*, the competition between the individualism of Henry's *areté* and the collectivism of *pietas* and "heroic martyrdom" swings between extremes. In his first engagement, Henry seems finally to give in to the standards of the group: "He suddenly lost concern for himself and forgot to look at a menacing fate. He became not a man but a member. He felt that something of which he was a part—a regiment, an army, a cause, or a country—was in crisis. He was welded into a common personality which was dominated by a single desire" (2:34). Soon, the group becomes even more important to him than the causes: "He felt the subtle battle brotherhood more potent even than the cause for which they were fighting. It was a mysterious fraternity" (2:35).

Much has been made of Henry's joining the subtle brotherhood, but few remember that when the enemy makes a second charge against the regiment, the mysterious fraternity dissolves under an individuality revived by Henry's sense of self-preservation. He turns tail and runs. Although Achilles has more grace and style, the effect is the same in either case: both Henry and Achilles desert their friends in the field. To say, as many do, that Henry should be damned for his desertion is to speak from an historically narrow perspective; from an Homeric standpoint, one cannot be so quick to judge. In fact, no moral judgments necessarily result from Henry's flight. If Henry can get away with it (he does), if no one finds out about it (no one does), and if later he can perform "great deeds" (he does), then that is all that matters. By the end of the sixth chapter, Henry's individualism, his Homeric sense, seems to have won a limited victory—victory because Henry has escaped being subsumed by the group, limited because his sense of shame dogs him throughout the novel.

In the novel's first half the battle for Henry's allegiance to Homeric or Christian-group values occurs in Henry's mind. In the first six chapters, Henry's conflicting feelings need little prodding; in the second six, the action of the novel intensifies, as do attacks on his individualism. In this quarter of the novel, Henry enters the "forest chapel," sees Jim Conklin die in a Christ-like way, and is mentally and verbally assaulted by the "tattered man." Here, too, he receives his "red badge of courage."

It should not be surprising in light of the epic structure that this section of *The Red Badge* is filled with religious imagery. Much critical ink has been spilt in a controversy over whether or not Crane, given his naturalistic bent and nihilist vision, intends Jim Conklin, for example, to represent Christ, or the tattered man to represent the Christian-group ideal; many feel that Crane himself was confused about it and that the novel fails because he fails to resolve the problem. From the standpoint of examining the traditional epic qualities of the book, there is no problem. These chapters mark what ultimately becomes a failure of the Christian-group value system—with two thousand years of indoctrination behind it—to make Henry Fleming return to the fold. It is not Crane's intent to have the reader see things in a religious way, but to see Henry succumb to the pathetic fallacy of Christian-colored glasses.

Arriving at a spot deep in the woods, Henry hears the trees "sing a hymn of twilight. . . . There was a lull in the noises of insects as if they had bowed their beaks and were making a devotional pause. There was silence save for the choruses of trees" (2:49). Henry now sees things through a "religious half light," and the forest seems to form a "chapel" complete with "arching boughs," "green doors," and a "brown carpet."

When Crane places more emphasis on character and action than upon natural scenes, Christian morality and group ethics are even more strongly merged. Both value systems require humility, love, awe, and admiration for something perceived as greater than and outside of the individual. In chapters six to twelve, the screw is tightened on Henry's conscience, demanding both complete subjection and unqualified support. The first person Henry sees after leaving the forest is the tattered man, who, for Henry, embodies the Christian-group ideal. The tattered man is introduced by a dignified and classical anaphora as if he were the subject of an ancient fable: "There was a tattered man. . . . " This archetypal follower listens to an officer's "lurid tale" with "much humility." Rough as the ragged private looks, his voice is as "gentle as a girl's," and when he speaks it is "timidly." His "pleading" eyes are described in a simile bearing a Christian symbol that could not have escaped Crane; they are "lamblike." With a general "air of apology in his manner," the tattered man is so humble, timid, and conventionally feminine that he becomes a caricature of a Christian-group member. Even his physiognomy betrays an overwhelming love for the group. "His homely face was suffused with a light of love for the army which was to him all things powerful and beautiful." Crane here takes standard emotional slither from the rhetoric of nineteenth-century religious writers' descriptions of people saved at camp meetings and attaches it to the army. All of the tattered man's questions are uttered "in a brotherly tone," and his "lean features wore an expression of awe and admiration." In short, he must have been meant to be a caricature, for even his breathing has in it a "humble admiration."[5]

It is also clear that Henry sees Jim Conklin in a "religious half light." Stallman's original reading of Conklin as Christ is fundamentally correct if one understands that it is Henry and not Crane who sees Conklin as Christ.[6] Few figures in American literature have a better claim to the trappings of Christ's Passion than does Jim Conklin. His initials are J. C., he is wounded in the side, he dies on a hill, he is a "devotee of a mad religion," and his death stirs "thoughts of a solemn ceremony." Those who deny that Conklin is a Christ-figure usually do so by pointing out that Conklin is a loud, cracker-crunching, rumormonger. Such evidence is specious, since these qualities are part of Jim only before he became "not a man but a member" by staying on the line during the battle.[7] Some also forget that Crane's intent is to show that Henry sees Conklin in this way, not that Conklin is that way.

One way to place the various episodes of the first half into a perspective of the moral and social competition between Christian-group values and the Homeric ideal of individualism (*areté*) may be to describe that epic competition as a representation of the psychology of Christian conversion from an egocentric individualism to an altruistic membership in the flock. The pattern is familiar; as a moral being, man in Christian process moves from the commission of sin to guilt, to alienation, to a desire for expiation, to confession, and finally to redemption.[8] In the end, the process fails to redeem Henry for Christianity, but it does give him a rough time of it, and it organizes the epic competition and psychology of the novel's first half.

Three particular episodes are representative of this psychological movement. The episodes with Mrs. Fleming, Jim Conklin, and the tattered man each appear to bring Henry steadily closer to rejecting his Homeric individuality while ultimately functioning ironically to force his acceptance of *areté*. By the time he is hit on the head and receives his "red badge of courage," Henry has sloughed off the Christian-group concept of heroism. His red badge is, however, not ironical in that he receives it for an act of cowardice; rather it is an outward sign—what the Greeks called *geras*—of his accomplishment in rejecting two thousand years of social and religious indoctrination. An epic feat.

Occurring in the first chapter, the "Mrs. Fleming" episode serves to increase Henry's feelings of sin and guilt over his Homeric sense of selfish individuality which encompasses egoism, insensitivity, and the pursuit of personal glory at all costs—*areté*. The episode opens with Henry in his hut (and *in medias res*) remembering his earlier thoughts about "breathless deeds," his "burning to enlist," and his having "despaired of witnessing a Greeklike struggle."

Mrs. Fleming is a stereotype of the pious, hard-working, long-suffering, farm boy's mother. Her views are Christian-group oriented and come from "deep conviction." Her "ethical motives" are "impregnable." Guilt and remorse over his insensitivity toward his mother work on Henry as he remembers a scene from his leave-taking: "When he had looked back from the gate, he had seen his mother kneeling among the potato parings. Her brown face, up-raised, was stained with tears, and her spare form was quivering" (2:7–8). The effect on Henry is predictable: "He bowed his head and went on, feeling suddenly ashamed of his purposes" (2:8). Significantly, he is not so much ashamed of enlisting as he is of his purposes, his longing for the glory road of individual heroism that scatters the hurt feelings and genuine needs of others along the roadside. Christians would accuse Henry of *hubris*; Augustan Romans would not chide him for enlisting but for having done so without thought to duty and family; Homeric Greeks would have wondered what all the fuss was about, shrugged their shoulders, and remarked that while the action might be a little sad, it was also probably necessary: how else become a hero? Unlike Homeric heroes, however, Henry leaves for war carrying in his soul the cultural burdens of twenty centuries of self-condemnation for succumbing to *areté*.

It is important to emphasize the universal qualities of the novel in general and of Henry Fleming in particular. He is at once common and uncommon; he is Man rebelling against his Mother, Mankind (or at least the archetypal American in the archetypal American novel) attempting to slough off the Past. In the American experience this last action ties Henry closely to the transcendental movement, as well as to such archetypal figures as Huck Finn, Natty Bumppo, Rip Van Winkle, and a host of other American heroes. The difference is that unlike Twain, Cooper, and Irving, Crane is using the formal epic ironically to destroy the traditions of heroism, and epic competition is used because its very purpose is to disparage what the past has considered to be the highest expression of man's duty, courage.

The Jim Conklin episode carries Henry a step further in the process by adding to sin and guilt the anguish of alienation and the desire for expiation through good works. After deserting the regiment and wandering through the forest, Henry joins a band of wounded men moving toward the rear. These men have stood their ground—for God and country possibly, for the group certainly. Their wounds seem to symbolize their sacrifices and their devotion to duty. Seeing them in this way, Henry feels alienated: "At times he regarded the wounded soldiers in an envious way. . . . He wished that he, too, had a wound, a red badge of courage" (2:54). Such a badge would grant to Henry membership and acceptance in the group, would assuage his guilt and close the gap between himself and the others caused by his alienation. Henry's anguish is now greater than during the earlier episode: "He felt his shame could be viewed. He was continually casting sidelong glances to see if the men were contemplating the letters of guilt he felt burned in his brow" (2:54). At this stage Henry is Stephen Crane's Dimmesdale, and the only difference between the two is that Crane's character ultimately is able to "put the sin at a distance." Hawthorne's protagonist never can.

Feeling that he bears the Mark of the Beast, Henry is then

confronted by Jim Conklin's wounds, and in his already anguished state, Henry is quite ready to see in Jim an exceptional Christian devotion to duty and sacrifice for the group. Jim's actions, however, deny Henry expiation and even serve further to heighten his anxiety. Henry's attempts to receive absolution are repulsed, for Jim only wants to be left alone to die: "The youth put forth anxious arms to assist him, but the tall soldier went firmly on as if propelled. . . . The youth had reached an anguish where the sobs scorched him. He strove to express his loyalty. . . . The youth wished his friend to lean upon him, but the other always shook his head and strangely protested. 'No—no—no—leave me be—leave me be—'. . . . and all the youth's offers he brushed aside" (2:56). Henry's view of Jim as a Christ is Henry's alone. The youth's attempts to assuage his guilt in a bath of atonement fail; although he asks, he does not receive—Jim Conklin will have none of it. All that remains is Henry's very real and painful desire for redemption. Redemption itself is as far away as ever.

Henry's Christian-group consciousness is pushed to its limits in the "tattered man" episode. There are two "sins" here: one is Henry's refusal to confess his earlier desertion of the regiment, and the other is his desertion of the tattered man, an act which redoubles his guilt. When Henry meets the tattered man, the latter repeatedly asks him, "Where yeh hit?" This question, asked over and over again, causes Henry to feel the "letters of guilt" burned, Dimmesdale-like, into his forehead. Instead of causing Henry to repent, however, the letters merely force him to desert the wounded tattered man and leave him to wander off into the fields to die. Immediately after deserting the tattered man, Henry's guilt reaches almost unbearable proportions: "The simple questions of the tattered man had been knife thrusts to him. They asserted a society that probes pitilessly at secrets until all is apparent. . . . He could not keep his crime concealed in his bosom. . . . He admitted that he could not defend himself" (2:62). Believing that "he envied those men whose bodies lay strewn" on the field, he explicitly wants to be redeemed: "A moral vindication was regarded by the youth as a very important thing" (2:67).

Confused, guilt-ridden, and afraid that the group may discover his "sin," Henry's mind goes through, as in the first chapter, the same metronomic movement between the demands of the group and the desires of the individual, but with more pain. Henry's anguish remains severe throughout the eleventh chapter. In the twelfth chapter, however, this changes.

Chapter 12 is the last chapter of the first half of *The Red Badge*. Like the end of the first half of the *Iliad*, the *Odyssey*, the *Aeneid*, *Paradise Lost*, and other epics, it includes both a culmination of the first half and a preparation for the second. In the twelfth book of the *Iliad*, the Trojans have broken into the Greek encampment. They are never again so close to victory. In the *Odyssey*, the hero nears the end of his wanderings and sets off in the next book for a final successful junket to Ithaca, where he will lay plans to set his house in order. In the *Aeneid*, Aeneas is about to land in Italy, thus putting himself in a position to fulfill his destiny by founding the Roman nation. In *Paradise Lost*, the battle in Heaven ends; Satan and his angels have fallen into Hell, and the stage is set for the second half: the fall of man. Similarly, in *The Red Badge*, Henry completes his epic of return by sloughing off his Christian-group conscience: he accepts his individuality, and he is then prepared to battle the group in the second half.

Henry is "reborn" after being hit on the head in chapter 12.[9] The language of the episode is carefully, even poetically, rendered to represent rebirth. After watching a group of retreating soldiers, Henry runs down from a rise, grabs one of the soldiers, and is clouted for his trouble:

[The other soldier] adroitly and fiercely swung his rifle. It crushed upon the youth's head. The man ran on.

The youth's fingers had turned to paste upon the other's arm. The energy was smitten from his muscles. He saw the flaming wings of lightning flash before his vision. There was a deafening rumble of thunder within his head.

Suddenly his legs seemed to die. He sank writhing to the ground. He tried to arise. In his efforts against the numbing pain he was like a man wrestling with a creature of the air.

There was a sinister struggle.

Sometimes he would achieve a position half erect, battle with the air for a moment, and then fall again, grabbing at the grass. His face was of a clammy pallor. Deep groans were wrenched from him.

At last, with a twisting movement, he got upon his hands and knees, and from thence, like a babe trying to walk, to his feet. . . . he went lurching over the grass.

He fought an intense battle with his body. His dulled senses wished him to swoon and he opposed them stubbornly, his mind portraying unknown dangers and mutilations if he should fall upon the field. He went tall soldier fashion. [2:70–71]

Structurally, the passage focuses first on the falling away of the old in a metaphorical death. Henry loses his sight, his hearing, and then his ability to stand erect. In the middle is a five-word, one-sentence paragraph describing a "sinister struggle" between life and death. From there, the reborn Henry gets up on his hands and knees "like a babe," and finally is able to walk. In spite of the almost allegorical nature of the passage, its essence remains one of a very physical, almost literal, and, most important, quite individual rebirth.

One cannot help but think that the anthropological cast of the passage is intentional. At least, it demonstrates that Crane, however unconsciously, was aware of the consequences for thought of the Darwinian revolution. For Henry, as for mankind, the traditional past could no longer provide solace. Indeed, as the second half of *The Red Badge* shows, the traditional past had to be rolled up and replaced by naturalism and impressionism. These terms, given Holton's appraisal of elements shared by definitions of the former and Nagel's definition of impressionism, can be seen in some lights as nearly synonymous and as twin effects of *Origin of the Species* and of the dissemination of other scientific discoveries.[10]

The action reported in this passage is unlike anything else in the book. Except for a later instance when he pushes another fellow, it is Henry's only hostile physical encounter in the novel. Certainly this is not Christian-group combat; it is especially unusual for those engaged in modern warfare. Prior to this point all battles have been described as remote from the individual. Cannons roar at each other, and men shoot at "vague forms" shifting and running through the smoke of many rifles. Always the action has been described in terms of one group charging toward or retreating from another. Moreover, his adversary fights under the same flag as Henry.

Here, for the first time, is a representation of a "Greeklike struggle" that once had been merely a part of Henry's dreams. It has not developed as Henry had expected, and may not be distinctly Homeric, but it is close to primitive hand-to-hand combat, and bears little resemblance to the "mighty blue machine" of the group. For the first time, Henry struggles with another man. Further, Henry's wound is unusual for participants in a modern, group war. Henry's wound is not from a bullet, but from the butt end of a modern weapon used as the most ancient of weapons; as one fellow observes, "It's raised a queer lump as if some feller lammed yeh on the head with a club" (2:77).

Henry's wandering off "tall soldier fashion" after receiving the blow on the head does not mean that Henry has been converted to a group view of things. To see Jim as a Christian-group figure is to make the same mistake Henry made. Strip away the dramatic symbolism of Henry's former vision of Conklin and one is left with a man dying, alone, unwilling to be helped, and as afraid of mutilation as any Homeric hero. Speech and action are "real"; Henry's interpretation of them may not be. When Henry thus goes "tall soldier fashion," it is not necessarily as a Christ-figure. Henry is in no shape at this point to interpret events; in this instance, the information comes directly from the narrator.[11] The dying Jim Conklin and the wounded Henry Fleming are linked, or seem to be linked, only by a desire to escape the group.

Wandering in the gathering darkness, Henry is finally given direction by an epic guide. Like the role of the captain in "The Reluctant Voyagers," the function of the "cheery man" is traditional to the machinery of epic. As Ariadne helps Theseus, Thetis comforts Achilles, Athena aids Odysseus, Venus supports and guides Aeneas, and Virgil leads Dante, so the cheery man helps Henry to gain self-control, and, as Gibson points out, places him in a position to confront those forces which he otherwise would have little power to oppose but which he must overcome in order to complete his epic task.[12] The cheery man leads Henry back to the regiment.

Unlike the two men in "The Reluctant Voyagers," Henry appreciates, albeit somewhat after the fact, the cheery man's help. And well he should, for as he staggers towards the campfires of his regiment in the beginning of the second half of *The Red Badge*, he has nearly done the impossible. In a sense, he has performed more courageously than Achilles. Peliades had only to reach his goal of *areté*, while Fleming had first to throw off his sense of sin and alienation. On one level, he has suffered all the slings and "arrows of scorn" that can be shot at an individual by the archers of conscience, guilt, and aliena-tion from the group. On another level, Henry has forced his way back through two millennia of nationalism and Christianity. Such an act is impossible for an ordinary man. To oppose and overcome, even to a limited degree, the teachings of secular and religious culture is an almost incredible, even epic, feat.

Outward Wars

Yet the battle is only half won. As the first twelve chapters are concerned with Henry's struggle to gain individuality of mind, the second half of *The Red Badge* concerns Henry's conflict with the same forces in the externalized, "outside" world. In terms of the epic of consciousness, the first half concerns Henry's escape from the cave, his coming to consciousness, and his gaining self-control, that is, coming to terms with alienation from the other—the group and the rest of the material world—and the fact of death. Having come to terms internally in the first half, he is ready to confront the other externally in the second half. Here, as in the *Aeneid*, the hero is confronted with a competition between his new-found values and an externalized embodiment and proponent of the value system he has recently overcome internally. In the second half of the *Aeneid*, Aeneas must confront, battle, and finally defeat the Roman version of the Homeric ideal of *areté* embodied in Turnus. In the last half of *The Red Badge*, Henry must confront, engage, and overcome Wilson, who has not only been "converted" and initiated into the group, but also has become the embodiment of Christian-group consciousness and its value system.

When Henry returns to confront the group, to enter into the midst of the "subtle brotherhood," he manages to resist its attempts to "initiate" him into membership. Henry seems aware at this point of the nature of this confrontation, because "there was a sudden sinking of his forces. He thought he must hasten to produce his tale to protect him from the missiles already at the lips of his redoubtable comrades." The "information" is a baldfaced lie: "Yes, yes. I've—I've had an awful time. I've been all over. Way over on the right. . . . I got separated from the regiment. Over on the right, I got shot. In the head. I never saw such fighting" (2:75–76). The lie works, and Henry seems to become the lost sheep returned to the fold.

Wilson, the sentinel who recognizes Henry staggering into camp, seems remarkably changed. Henry now views Wilson much as he had viewed the tattered man, only with colder eyes. In the first chapter, Wilson acted the part of a *miles gloriosus*, a parody of Achilles. In that chapter, which mirrors the first book of the *Iliad*, Wilson engaged Jim Conklin in an argument. Like Achilles and Agamemnon, "they came near to fighting over" their differences. Wilson also spent much time bragging about his prowess in battle. Now, however, Wilson seems to embody Christian-group values. When first seen in chapter 13, he is standing guard over the regiment. Upon recognizing Henry, he lowers his rifle and welcomes the youth back: "There was husky emotion in his voice" (2:75). Later, while dressing Henry's wound, Wilson acts out the feminine role of the soothing and clucking mother hen who welcomes one of her lost chicks back to the coop: "He had the bustling ways of an amateur nurse. He fussed around" (2:78). When Wilson puts his cloth on Henry's head, it feels to the youth "like a tender woman's hand" (2:79).[13]

Because he didn't run, Wilson was subsumed by that "regiment, army, cause," or country; he joined the "subtle brotherhood," the "mysterious fraternity born of the smoke and danger of death." At the beginning of the battle neither Henry nor Wilson had gained a genuine sense of individuality; both at that point were vulnerable to the group. Because he ran, Henry was excluded from the ego-annihilating forces which Wilson joined.

As a result, Henry and Wilson are now two very different

kinds of men. Wilson, who had earlier jumped at any chance to get into an argument or a fight, now stops a fight between two men; he explains to Henry, "I hate t' see th' boys fightin' 'mong themselves" (2:84). Henry, however, feels no such obligation to become a peacemaker; he laughs and reminds Wilson of an earlier fight the formerly loud soldier had had with "that Irish feller." Certain that he would be killed, Wilson had given Henry a packet of letters before the first battle with instructions that they be sent home after his "imminent" death. The contrast between Wilson's new-found humility and Henry's arrogance appears when Wilson asks for the letters back. Wilson flushes and fidgets, "suffering great shame." When Henry gives them back, he tries "to invent a remarkable comment upon the affair. He could conjure up nothing of sufficient point. He was compelled to allow his friend to escape unmolested with his packet. And for this he took unto himself considerable credit. It was a generous thing. . . . The youth felt his heart grow more strong and stout. He had never been compelled to blush in such a manner for his acts; he was an individual of extraordinary virtues" (2:87). There is a double irony here. On one level, the passage mocks Henry, but on another, Henry is essentially correct. He has not been "compelled" to undergo the humility of confession. He has overcome in large measure the need for communal redemption of guilt and shame. He does, indeed, have extraordinary "virtues," but they are the "virtues" of *areté*, pride, and individualism.

As they begin the second day of battle, Henry and Wilson are very soon recognized by the group as entirely different kinds of heroes. First, Henry is transfigured by *menos*, the animallike battle-rage of Homeric heroes: "Once, he, in his intent hate, was almost alone and was firing when all those near him ceased. He was so engrossed in his occupation that he was not aware of a lull" (2:96). One man derides him for not stopping when the others had, but the lieutenant (whose "voice" had been described as expressing a "divinity") praises Henry in animistic terms: "By heavens, if I had ten thousand wild-cats like you I could tear th' stomach outa this war in less'n a week!" (2:97). Finally, Henry receives the recognition from the group that Homeric heroes seek. He is viewed as someone separate, distinct, and most important, superior: "They now looked upon him as a war-devil" (2:97), they are "awe-struck."

Wilson is a hero of a different age. Henry does not incite the group to action; his only concern is for his own heroism. Wilson, the hero of the group, serves this purpose: "The friend of the youth aroused. Lurching suddenly forward and dropping to his knees, he fired an angry shot at the persistent woods. This action awakened the men. They huddled no more like sheep . . . they began to move forward" (2:106–7).

Wilson has become the leader of his flock, and Henry has become an Homeric "war devil."

There are a number of confrontations between Henry and Wilson in their respective roles as individual and group heroes. The morning after Henry's return to camp, for example, Wilson "tinkers" with the bandage on Henry's head, trying to keep it from slipping. Friendly, consoling, and helpful, Wilson is berated by an unfriendly, arrogant Henry: "Gosh-dern it' . . . you're the hangdest man I ever saw! You wear muffs on your hands. Why in good thunderation can't you be more easy? . . . Now, go slow, an' don't act as if you was nailing down carpet." Henry seems already to have gained superiority over his counterpart: "He glared with insolent command at his friend" (2:81).

Later, when Henry remembers the letters Wilson had given him, he again feels his superiority and thinks in terms of dominance: "He had been possessed of much fear of his friend, for he saw how easily questionings could make holes in his feelings. . . . He now rejoiced in the possession of a small weapon with which he could prostrate his comrade at the first signs of cross-examination. He was master" (2:85). Wilson remains a symbol to Henry of Christian-group conscience throughout the second half, and Henry never completely overcomes his own Christian-group sense. It dogs him.

The crucial confrontation between the two heroes is a face-to-face physical encounter on the battlefield. It occurs, fittingly, in a contest to determine who will carry the flag across the field in the charge. For Wilson, the traditional approach to the flag as a symbol of a group is most appropriate. Possession of the flag would mean that Wilson had reached the goal of all group epic heroes: to become the idealized symbol of the group. For Henry, the flag is also a symbol of the group. But Homeric heroes strive after *geras*, the prize, the symbol by which they are acknowledged by the group as superior. Possession of the flag would mean that he had fulfilled the aspect of *areté* that demands that he achieve supremacy over the group. Consequently, the flag becomes for Henry "a goddess, radiant, that bent its form with an imperious gesture to him. It was a woman . . . that called to him with the voice of his hopes" (2:108).

Since the flag is a symbol both for the group and for the superior individual, it is natural, when the bearer is shot, that both Henry and Wilson should go after the flag. It is also inevitable, although slightly contrived, that they should reach it at the same time: "He [Henry] made a spring and a clutch at the pole. At the same instant, his friend grabbed it from the other side" (2:108).

Neither Henry nor Wilson relinquishes the flagpole and a "small scuffle" ensues. For Henry, however, possession of the flag means so much in terms of dominance over his peers that he has no compunctions about using force against his comrade: "The youth roughly pushed his friend way" (2:110).

In gaining the flag, Henry has defeated his Christian-group rival and the value system Wilson champions. Henry has gained supremacy over his peers, achieving his *areté*. Yet the victory is not complete: there is still the enemy's flag. Were Henry to claim that flag as well, he would be proven superior not only to his peers, but also to the collective body. Henry fails. Although there is much heroism in becoming individual, one is never completely freed from the group. Its influences, physical and mental, remain forever. Although Henry has equaled or surpassed the deeds of Achilles and Odysseus, although he has overcome in large measure the long stony sleep of Christian-group culture and heritage, he fails to gain a complete victory. It is as if Henry knows what its possession would mean: "The youth had centered the gaze of his soul upon that other flag. Its possession would be high pride" (2:129). But Wilson, that champion of the group, had dogged Henry across the battlefield and beat Henry to it by springing like Christ the Panther:[14] "The youth's friend . . . sprang at the flag as a panther at prey. He pulled at it, and wrenching it free, swung up its red brilliancy with a mad cry of exultation" (2:130).

In terms of the epic tradition, Henry's possessing the other flag could have meant possibly a complete victory for the Homeric epic over the social epic after two thousand years. It might also have meant a winning back of the heroic, individual "soul" after two millennia of suppression by Christian-group value systems, both political and spiritual. But, as the later Scratchy Wilson of "The Bride Comes to Yellow Sky" and the Swede of "The Blue Hotel" discover, such a victory is fleeting at best and always illusory. Wilson may have lost an individual encounter with Henry, but he has also proven that the group cannot be completely defeated by the individual.

Victories

The epic tradition demands that a writer replace former concepts of epic heroism with his own if he wishes to be more than
a mere imitator. In nearly all of Crane's best work, his idea of
heroism is his ideal of personal honesty. Repeatedly, Crane
measures his characters against this standard; Henry Fleming
measures as well as any.

More than any other sort of writer, one whose work has epic
dimensions lends to his fictional heroes his own supreme
ambition; so much is this so, in fact, that the poet himself may
be considered the ultimate hero of his own epic, and is sometimes difficult to separate from the fictional hero. For millennia
the epic poet has been set apart from his fellows by his abilities,
but especially by the intensity of his vision and by the degree to
which he believes in it. For Crane, keeping close to his vision,
in terms both of apprehension and of comprehension, is the
standard not only of honesty but of heroism as well.

The desire to see clearly runs through *The Red Badge of
Courage*. Henry in particular seeks continually to perceive with
his own eyes. There are more than two hundred references in
The Red Badge to Henry seeing, not seeing, or trying to see.
However, his sight tends always to be obscured either by the
group, which limits what the individual can see, or by a kind of
Homeric hero complex in which Henry feels that an individual
can see everything. Each is a form of blindness and each
corresponds to one of the two epic value systems. There is an
implication throughout most of the novel (the implication
becomes explicit in the last chapter) that history is little more
than an individual interpretation of events raised to a level of
cultural reporting and collective interpreting. Both as individual and as representative man, Henry makes his own
specific interpretations of events. On the other hand, those
interpretations are also colored by epic concepts. If the indi-

vidual's interpretation is deluded, so is the epic's, and vice-versa.

Since Crane uses "vision" as a metaphor for his own particular notion of heroism, former notions of epic heroism are first debased and then replaced by the use of images and references to seeing. One of the value systems attacked in *The Red Badge* is the Christian-group view, which obscures and distorts the attempts of the individual to "see." The group, in the form of the army or the brigade or the regiment, is constantly associated with smoke or fog. As Henry is about to move into his first engagement, he identifies the fog with the army; indeed, the fog seems to emanate from the group: "The youth thought the damp fog of early morning moved from the rush of a great body of troops" (2:22). The same image is used in the opening sentence of the novel: "The cold passed reluctantly from the earth, and the retiring fogs revealed an army stretched out on the hills, resting" (2:3). Smoke is even more often associated with the group. Although realistic in a novel about war before the invention of smokeless powder, the image is used for much more than verisimilitude. At one point the position of an entire brigade is identified only by reference to the position of a blanket of smoke: "A brigade ahead of them went into action with a rending roar. It was as if it had exploded. And, thereafter, it lay stretched in the distance behind a long gray wall that one was obliged to look twice at to make sure that it was smoke" (2:28). Not only is smoke identified with the brigade, but smoke also seems to give it protection.

The group is also seen in terms of darkness, snakes, and monsters, which in epics and archetypes of the unconscious are usually identified with evil. As the army is forming to march into battle, Henry perceives the group: "From off in the darkness, came the trampling of feet. The youth could occasionally see dark shadows that moved like monsters" (2:15). As the "monsters" moved off in columns, "there was an occasional flash and glimmer of steel from the backs of all these huge crawling reptiles" (2:15). And the "two long, thin, black columns" appear "like two serpents crawling from the cavern of the night" (2:16). The men of the group themselves sometimes appear "satanic" (2:18) to Henry.

Most often, however, the smoke of the group obscures and distorts Henry's vision. With the smoke of "the war atmosphere" around him in his first engagement, Henry had "a sensation that his eye-balls were about to crack like hot stones" (2:35). His desire to see is constantly getting in the way of his assimilation into the group, but he can never get an unobstructed view and his other senses are stifled, almost annihilated by the physical and metaphorical "smoke" of the group. Against this smoke Henry directs more of his anger than against a charging enemy: "Buried in the smoke of many rifles his anger was directed not so much against the men whom he knew were rushing toward him as against the swirling battle phantoms which were choking him, stuffing their smoke robes down his parched throat" (2:35).

The group has the ability to hide reality from the individual. The group takes away the individual's unobstructed use of his senses—the only means he has of perceiving the world around him. While surrounded by "smoke," a man cannot "see," and will behave in the way the group wants him to behave. Shortly before Henry becomes "not a man but a member," for example, he and the regiment are moving rapidly forward to a "struggle in the smoke": "In this rush they were apparently all deaf and blind" (2:31).

After he has run, been hit on the head, and returned to the group, Henry sees the regiment in a more sinister aspect. After spending the night in sleep Henry awakes and it seems to him "that he had been asleep for a thousand years" (2:68). This "sleep," of course, takes him back in time, not forward, and so he sees "gray mists," and around him "men in corpse-like hues" with "limbs . . . pulseless and dead." If every epic hero must visit hell, then, for Henry, being in the middle of the group is just that: he sees "the hall of the forest as a charnel place. He believed for an instant that he was in the house of the dead" (2:80).

If the group influence which Henry has resisted and over which he has gained some dominance causes the individual to see less than he is able, the Homeric view of man purports to allow the individual to "see" more than he actually can. Crane renders the Homeric view meaningless by showing that it too is clouded. That is, if Wilson, the group hero, is given "new eyes" and now apparently sees himself as a "wee thing" (2:82), then Henry, the Homeric hero, becomes so caught up in his individual desires that his eyes are reduced to "a glazed vacancy" (2:96). He becomes a "barbarian, a beast" (2:97). He sees himself as a "pagan who defends his religion" (2:97), and he sees his battle-rage as "fine, wild, and, in some ways, easy. He had been a tremendous figure, no doubt. By this struggle he had overcome obstacles which he had admitted to be mountains. They had fallen like paper peaks, and he was now what he called a hero" (2:97).

The whole of chapter 17 describes Henry as being in the grip of the blind battle-rage of Homeric heroes. He forgets that he is merely a private engaged in a small charge on one day of one battle. He thinks of himself as colossal in size and of the other soldiers as "flies sucking insolently at his blood" (2:95). Although his neck is "bronzed" and he fires his rifle with a fierce grunt as if he were "dealing a blow of the fist with all his strength" (2:96), he is essentially what one soldier calls this "war devil": "Yeh infernal fool" (2:96). Heroic Henry certainly is, even in a traditional way, but a bit foolish as well.

Henry soon gains a truer vision. Going with Wilson to get

some water, Henry, as well as his image of himself as a
Homeric hero, is deflated by a "jangling general" who refers to
Henry's regiment, and implicitly to Henry himself, as a lot of
"mule drivers" (2:101). Henry, who had earlier viewed nature
as a sympathetic goddess in language filled with Virgilian
pathetic fallacy and Christian symbolism (the forest-chapel,
for example), and later as a capricious, sometimes malevolent
beast much as Homer saw it, now has "new eyes" and sees
himself as "very insignificant" (2:101). This is not necessarily a
Christian sense of insignificance, nor even a completely naturalistic one, but simply a realization that compared with more
powerful forces, including the regiment, he is powerless.
Moreover, since officers are often associated with gods, the
sun, and other natural and supernatural entities, Henry's
discovery can be seen as developing from his earlier views of
nature.[15]

After discovering his insignificance, Henry is in a position to
receive a new heroism, a new vision, a "real" vision. In his
charge across the field on the second day of battle, it "seemed
to the youth that he saw everything":

*Each blade of the green grass was bold and clear. He thought that he
was aware of every change in the thin, transparent vapor that floated
idly in sheets. The brown or gray trunks of the trees showed each
roughness of their surfaces. And the men of the regiment, with their
starting eyes and sweating faces, running madly, or falling, as if
thrown headlong, to queer, heaped up corpses—all were compre-
hended. His mind took a mechanical but firm impression, so that
afterward everything was pictured and explained to him, save why he
himself was there. [2:105]*

A "mechanical" impression of some blades of grass, tree
trunks, and sweating, frightened, dying men: that is all one
can ever hope to see. The process of epic has been reversed.

Virgil had expanded Homer's view of ten or twenty years of glory on the plains before a small town in Asia Minor to include a long-lived empire encompassing the known world. Similarly, the Christian epics of Charlemagne and the crusades are described as world wars. Milton extended the epic beyond human time and farther out than human space. Crane doubled back upon the epic tradition, gradually narrowing space until the epic vision includes only a minute perception and compressing time until that perception exists only for a fleeting instant. It is epical in its achievement and heroic only because Crane has shown it to be the only vision possible for man that remains "bold and clear."

Tiny but unobscured by the smoke of the group or the blinding *menos* of *areté*, Henry's vision has made him Crane's version of the best epic hero. Trying to "observe everything" in his first battle, but failing to "avoid trees and branches," Henry now sees only *something*. Gone is the Roman vision of national destiny and the Miltonic perception of a Puritan God's universe. Heroism is defined in *The Red Badge* as one man's limited but perhaps illusionless vision: grass blades, tree trunks, dying men.

This vision has dominated the literature of the twentieth century and has allowed writers who followed Crane to make the first tentative steps toward a new supreme fiction based upon consciousness of a materialistic universe while discarding the old fictions based upon the imagination. It is upon this vision that Wallace Stevens, for example, built his poetic edifice, and it is because of the new tradition inaugurated by *The Red Badge* that Stevens could write that "in the presence of the violent reality of war, consciousness takes the place of the imagination."[16] That is precisely what happens in this novel.

The epic of consciousness in *The Red Badge* is clearly set forth. Henry begins the novel in his hut, emblem of the enclosed violence of his mind. In this enclosure, cluttered by cracker boxes, clothing, and utensils, he gives vent to his cluttered and conflicting fears and anxieties. "Convicted by himself of many shameful crimes against the gods of tradition" (2:14) and feeling "alone in space," he has "visions of a thousand tongued fear," and admits that "he would not be able to cope with this monster" (2:20). When he first goes into combat, he sees "that it would be impossible for him to escape from the regiment. It enclosed him. And there were iron laws of tradition and laws on four sides. He was in a moving box" (2:23). After escaping from the regimental enclosure, he enters a succession of archetypes for the unconscious—the forest, a swamp, "deep thickets"—each enclosing those which follow, until he reaches "a place where the high, arching boughs made a chapel" (2:47). Here is a different sort of cave, for this is not at first the enclosure of unconscious fears, nor an enclosure of transcendence, but rather a false cave, like the den of Error (book 1, canto 1) and the cave of Mammon (book 2, canto 7) in the *Faerie Queene*, where the hero is lured toward a false transcendence. In Henry's case the promise comes in the form of religious transcendentalism. While the insects are praying and the trees are whispering, Henry pushes open the "green doors" and enters the chapel. In a paragraph or two Crane both anticipates W. W. Hudson and Edgar Rice Burroughs and parodies the Schianatulander and chapel scenes of *Parzival*, for Henry has no sooner entered and is standing "near the threshold," when "he stopped horror-stricken at the sight of the thing."

He was being looked at by a dead man who was seated with his back against a column-like tree. The corpse was dressed in a uniform that once had been blue but now was faded to a melancholy shade of green. The eyes, staring at the youth, had changed to the dull hue to be seen on the side of a dead fish. The mouth was opened. Its red had changed

to an appalling yellow. Over the grey skin of the face ran little ants.
One was trundling some sort of a bundle along the upper lip. [2:47]

The stark clarity of this paragraph, with its excruciatingly painful materialism, provides a perfect contrast to the "religious half-light" leading up to this description. While the description is faintly reminiscent of Thoreau's mock epic paragraphs on ants in *Walden*, its main purpose seems to be to pose starkly the problem that Henry and other epic heroes must face. Somehow, the pathetic fallacy, the religious rose-colored glasses, must be removed, and Henry must still be able to face the "thing"—the fact of death. At this early stage, the contrast is too great for Henry and he responds by screaming and fleeing from the enclosure, which promised transcendence but delivered only death. Another way of saying it is that he was lulled by the imagination and then confronted by pure consciousness. He heads back to the regiment. Only later, after facing death in the field, does Henry accept a classical, almost Lucretian materialism with respect to mortality.[17] This seems to be what Henry learns: "He knew that he would no more quail before his guides wherever they should point. He had been to touch the great death and found that, after all, it was but the great death" (2:135).

Before this, however, Henry has other caves to face. It may be said that after he crosses the river in chapter 3, Henry is subterranean for nearly the remainder of the novel, much as Dante is throughout the *Inferno*. The others are merely caves within caves, hells within Hades. One of these is the night camp of the regiment in chapter 13. Here Henry catches "glimpses of visages that loomed pallid and ghostly, lit with a phosphorescent glow" (2:77). Another enclosure of failed transcendence, this camp is like that to which the captain brings the reluctant voyagers. This too contains a window on the stars: "Far off to the right, through a window in the forest could be seen a handful of stars" (2:77). Managing to resist the temptations of even this "charnel house," Henry subsequently overcomes the numerous enclosures formed by the smoke of the regiment's many rifles and achieves his "bold and clear" vision.

Defeats

The latest episode in the long controversy about the quality of *The Red Badge* begins with Henry Binder's 1978 articles and 1979 edition of Crane's novel for *The Norton Anthology of American Literature*—articles in which he proposes restoring, and an edition in which he does restore, several manuscript passages to the printed text. Restoring these passages, Binder claims, makes a muddled novel clear and consistent. The controversy regarding whether or not Henry "grows" is resolved: he does not; the novel is clearly ironic. While agreeing that the original Appleton edition poses problems, Donald Pizer contends that the traditional text is the best we have until evidence stronger than Binder's appears. Pizer takes issue with Binder on essentially two points: first, that because there is no evidence suggesting that Crane was pressured into making the cuts, it can only be assumed that he freely chose to make them; and second, that Binder errs in assuming that "a clear and consistent novel is better than an ambivalent and ambiguous one."[18]

Because it involves an entire chapter, the longest of Binder's additions must be addressed in some detail by anyone discussing the structure of *The Red Badge*. This is especially true of a discussion of classical epic structure, where arithmetical divisions are significant and the notion of a twenty-five-chapter epic poses some problems. The restored chapter is the original manuscript's chapter twelve, coming after the Appleton chapter eleven. Traditional epics are structurally divided in half. A twenty-five-chapter novel based on epic would be divided somewhere near the middle of chapter thirteen, leaving twelve and a half chapters on either side. Chapter thirteen in the new Norton edition is chapter twelve of the traditional Appleton edition. The middle of this chapter describes Henry receiving his wound, a description already discussed as pivotal to the work. Since Henry is in no position to do much on his own between the time he is wounded (the middle of the Norton) and the time the Cheery man deposits him with the regiment (ending the traditional text's first half), the different editions have little effect on the validity of the novel's epic structure.

The content of the added chapter does little more than reaffirm the metronomic quality of Henry's thoughts and emotions as they move between extremes of Nietzschean egotism and Paulean self-flagellation. On one hand, "it was always clear to the youth that he was entirely different from other men; that his mind had been cast in a unique mold. Hence laws that might be just to ordinary men, were, when applied to him, peculiar and galling outrages."[19] On the other hand, when "his mind pictured the death of Jim Conklin" and in it "he saw the shadows of his fate," he felt himself to be "unfit": "He did not come into the scheme of further life. His tiny part had been played and he must go."[20]

The additions appearing in the 1979 Norton edition of *The Red Badge* do little to enhance or diminish the notion of *The Red Badge* as having structural and thematic roots in classical epic. At the same time, since the passages do little more than reaffirm the greatness of *The Red Badge*, the classical dicta of economy and simplicity ought to apply, and one giving a supposedly classical reading of a work ought to side with his sources.

The final chapter of *The Red Badge* presents perhaps the greatest critical problem in the Crane canon. Many of the critical reservations about Crane's importance and abilities rest in the complexities and supposed inconsistencies (even inanities) of this chapter.[21]

The last chapter is both complete and consistent. It is a deliberate reversal of all that has gone before. Throughout the largest portion of *The Red Badge*, Henry is in the process of sloughing off both the Christian-group "walking-sticks" of Stallman's interpretation and the Homeric "creeds" of this reading. If the final chapter of *The Red Badge* is naturalistic, it is so only within the context of Crane's conception of the epic.

That a man may learn and then forget, as Holton says, pervades Crane's writings; in terms of the epic nature of *The Red Badge*, a man may forget and then remember. In the first twenty-three chapters, Henry proceeds to "forget" all previous cultural notions and epic concepts about the way life is. Having "forgotten," he finally achieves an impressionistic vision of the individual man unencumbered by epic and cultural trappings. In the final chapter, however, Henry "remembers"; his former epic value systems sweep back over him, and he is left at the end dreaming dreams he had dreamt in the beginning.

Throughout twenty-three chapters of the novel the major concern is to discover the true nature of heroism. In the final chapter, however, all epic values are specifically refuted. Because he forgets the vision that he has found, and the limited heroism he has discovered, Henry becomes a nonhero. *The Red Badge*, too, is negated, a nonepic. Unlike Milton, Virgil, and Homer, Crane does not wait for his particular notion of heroism to be satirized by others; he mocks it himself.[22]

The Red Badge of Courage ends by mocking the epic genre and its heroic ideals. But the novel, so saturated with epic tradition, cannot be exiled from the epic province. Its exploitation of epic conventions attests to the lingering vitality of the genre, but its annihilation of heroism—Homeric, Virgilian, Catholic, or Miltonic—at the same time exposes the genre's vulnerability.

The novel marks a transition from the formal epic tradition to all that is Homerically nonepic in modern fiction: triumphant chaos and successful deceit.

The last chapter is an ironic recapitulation of each epic value system present in the remainder of the book. Homeric *areté* is savagely mocked, as is Christian-group heroism. The primary target, however, is that final concept of heroism, Crane's own, which Henry has achieved earlier: that concept based only on the individual's ability to peer into the pit of reality with a gaze unclouded by cultural and epic notions of what the world is like. Throughout this final chapter, Henry's (and Crane's) perception-based, impressionistic heroism is mocked by means of an ironic significance attached to images of and references to the sense of sight. Henry enters the chapter a cleareyed hero; he exits blind and deluded.

As the chapter opens, the battle has begun to wane and the sounds of war have begun "to grow intermittent and weaker." Henry's newfound vision soon runs the gamut of perception from egotistical pride to cringing guilt and humility, and is, in effect, also becoming "weaker." As the regiment begins to "retrace its way" like a snake "winding off in the direction of the river," Henry is with it, recrossing the Stygian stream he had crossed in chapter 3. Similarly, Henry's mind is "undergoing a subtle change": "It took moments for it to cast off its battleful ways and resume its accustomed course of thought. Gradually his brain emerged from the clogged clouds and at last he was enabled to more closely comprehend himself and his circumstance" (2:133). After "his first thoughts were given to rejoicings" because he had "escaped" the battle, Henry's vision becomes distorted. First, he contemplates his "achievements." With Homeric eyes he sees his deeds as "great and shining." His deluded vision is so distorted that he dresses those deeds in the royal "wide purple and gold," which, on Henry, give off sparkles "of various deflections."

Next, he assumes Christian eyes, and his visions of Homeric glory, of *areté*, are destroyed by an exaggerated guilt brought on by the memory of his crime against the tattered man. The tattered man had tormented his unmercifully, but all Henry sees is a grotesquely distorted image of the gentle tattered man transmogrified into a weird Christian version of some apostle of revenge who visits on Henry a "vision of cruelty." One delusion displaces another, so that Henry's previous vision, as well as his heroism, becomes changed and meaningless, because no longer is it his alone. Homeric pride makes Henry a strutting fool, and Christian-group guilt betrays him as a coward.

Images of and references to vision provide further ironic commentary on the quality of "perception" inherent in the two traditional epic value systems. For example, Crane mocks three specific aspects of *areté* in the final chapter by proving them to be false or wildly exaggerated visions of reality. The first mocks the lack of any firm moral sense in the ancient Greek battle code. At times, Henry has done less than his *areté* demands of him, but he rightly ignores this when contemplating his great deeds and he even feels "gleeful and unregretting." Another aspect of *areté* mocked by Crane is the all-important result of the Homeric hero's desire for glory, "public recognition of his *areté*: it runs through Greek life."[23] Henry tends to exaggerate the quality of his *areté*, and consequently the recognition it deserves, in a sort of daydream vision, a "procession of memory" in which "his public deeds were paraded in great and shining prominence" (2:133). The final mockery concerns that aspect of heroism lying at the heart of *areté*: the recognition of the hero's superiority over his peers. If we remember the soldier's comic, even ridiculous speech concerning "Flem's" bravery and the somewhat qualifying and dubiously conferred title "jimhickey," Henry's recollections seem to be all out of proportion: "He recalled with a thrill of joy

the respectful comments of his fellows upon his conduct"
(2:134).

Henry's progression toward heroism during the first twenty-three chapters reverses and inverts itself in the last chapter,
for Henry's vision is a distortion that destroys his notion of
Homeric bravery and of *areté*. Henry's semi-sin of leaving the
tattered man haunts him.[24] Crane here employs a parody of
nineteenth-century Protestant tracts, much as he has described Henry's Homeric deeds in the language traditionally
used to depict the victory marches of great warriors: "A spec-
ter of reproach came to him. There loomed the dogging memory of the tattered soldier—he who gored by bullets and faint
for blood, had fretted concerning an imagined wound in
another; he who had loaned his last of strength and intellect
for the tall soldier; he who, blind with weariness and pain, had
been deserted in the field" (2:134). Henry is then "followed"
by a "vision of cruelty" which clings "near to him always" and
darkens "his view of these deeds in purple and gold." This
"somber phantom" heightens Henry's guilt; he becomes
"afraid it would stand before him all his life." Thus, "he saw
his vivid error." After recognizing that he had sinned, Henry
receives partial expiation in the form of partial forgetfulness:
"Yet he gradually mustered force to put the sin at a distance.
And at last his eyes seemed to open to some new ways. He
found that he could now look back upon the brass and bombast of his earlier gospels and see them truly. He was gleeful
when he discovered that he now despised them" (2:135).
Henry here exchanges one false view of himself for another.
The Homeric vision has given way to a Christian-group one.
Crane, with beautiful, lyric irony, moves Henry away from the
war and from the battle in his mind: "So it came to pass that as
he trudged from the place of blood and wrath his soul
changed" (2:135). Henry now believes that "the world was a
world for him," as a Christian-group hero should.

There is yet another way, however, in which Crane sets about to destroy the epic. By ironically disparaging the epic view of man's history, Crane ridicules the concept that readers have of the epic genre. The epic has long been one of the more revered forms of historical interpretation and cultural expression. Through epic poetry Homer presents man as a godlike animal struggling to gain a measure of immortality through the public recognition of great deeds. But the Homeric man was like Lear in the storm—alone, naked, and "unaccommodated"—and this is probably why Crane preferred this view more than other traditional views: it was closer to his notion, expressed in "The Blue Hotel," that "conceit is the very engine of life." Virgil gave man more hope by giving him the opportunity to identify and merge with the immortality of a national group. By interpreting history in terms of a great empire, he was also in some measure espousing a kind of immortality. Medieval and Renaissance epic, including *The Song of Roland* and Tasso's *Gerusalemme liberata*, glorified the church militant, ordained to victory. Milton went even farther. He regarded man as completely unworthy of immortality, but acknowledged man's hope in a merciful God's love; man's earthly history spans the interval between creation and final redemption.

Crane felt that these interpretations of history were, to one degree or another, part of a giant hoax willfully perpetrated on man by man. At times he could be downright Aeschylean: "Hope," as Berryman quotes him, "is the most vacuous emotion of mankind."

The Red Badge is a denial of the epic view of history, which Crane felt creates an absurd, illusory, and vacuous emotion.

In the first twenty-three chapters of *The Red Badge* an epic fable is presented which carries the reader back through history. Henry begins *in medias res*, confused and torn between the two major epic views of history, and between two epic value systems as they have filtered through the epic into and out of culture. One of Henry's great accomplishments is his success in throwing off, if only for a short time, the Christian-group view that has dominated the long history of the social epic—indeed of all intellectual life in the West. Next, Henry rejects the rest of history, as recorded by the individual epic, by sloughing off the hope of being an immortal, Homeric "war devil." Finally, past all Christian doctrine, beyond the emotional slither of patriotism and breast-beating brass and bombast, this young man finds a vision in some blades of grass and the grooved bark of a few trees. He is, for an instant, free as few have ever been free; he is loosed from the illusions of history. Perhaps, because it is so limited in duration, Crane is mocking his own illusion, and that of Americans from Franklin to Ginsberg, that man can indeed throw off the process of history and the illusions it etches into the brain.

However, those twenty-three chapters may not be a fairy-tale epic. Crane may have felt that through catalytic and catastrophic experiences like war, man can scrape the scales of history from his eyes. Perhaps all the teachings of history are reduced to absurdity in the midst of the immense experience, if one tries hard enough to see for himself. Perhaps one can universalize Crane's statement that "a man is only responsible for the personal quality of his honesty" of vision. "A man is sure to fail at it," he said, "but there is something in the failure." Although the paucity of the vision may make it ironic, there is some heroism involved in the sheer ability to perceive reality. In either case, however, the last chapter of the novel indicates that Crane felt heroism to be impossible beyond the immediacy of experience.

This aspect of the last chapter functions by way of a metaphorical equation: memory is to the individual as history is to the species. As Henry moves away from the immediate experience, his memory creates lies and delusions about that experience. The ironic laughter from Crane results from his belief that man cannot really learn from experience, even when he can reach an illusionless view of reality through that experience. Once it is over, once one is no longer staring at the face of red death, then memory, or history, distorts that experience all out of any recognizable proportion.

In the last chapter, history becomes what memory becomes —a mechanism for man to build his self-image. Through the two main thrusts of the history of Western civilization, as expressed by the epic genre, man is deluded into believing himself to be either more or less than he actually is. In the end, Henry is led by his memory to believe with conviction all the mad, distorted hopes of epic history. Ironically, "at last his eyes opened on some new ways" (2:135). These are new ways only for Henry; they are as old as history. Darwin mounted on Mather.

These "new ways" are a collation of Homeric and Christian-group values. There is still much pride in Henry, but also much humility. Together, they form a paradoxically proud humility: "He felt a quiet man-hood, non-assertive but of sturdy and strong blood" (2:135). The sum of Henry's wisdom, apparently gained from these seemingly "new" ways, and required of epic heroes, is expressed in what becomes, upon close examination, a meaningless platitude worthy of the climax of a dime-novel adventure: "He had been to touch the great death, and found that, after all, it was but the great death. He was a man" (2:135).

The final delusion of history and memory Crane repudiated is that of "hope." Part of the reason that Virgil and Milton wrote epics was to give men hope. Beautifully parodic, and powerfully ironic, the last paragraphs of *The Red Badge* express the hopes of Aeneas and Adam, of Columbus and Hiawatha, and of people at all times and in all places, hot to cool, hard to soft, pain to pleasure, hell to heaven:

So it came to pass that as he trudged from the place of blood and wrath, his soul changed. He had come from hot-ploughshares to prospects of clover tranquility and it was as if hot-ploughshares were not. Scars faded as flowers.

It rained. The procession of weary soldiers became a bedraggled train, despondent and muttering, marching with churning effort, in a trough of liquid brown mud under a low, wretched sky. Yet the youth smiled, for he saw that the world was a world for him though many discovered it to be made of oaths and walking-sticks. . . . The sultry nightmare was in the past. He had been an animal blistered and sweating in the heat and pain of war. He turned now with a lover's thirst, to images of tranquil skies, fresh meadows, cool brooks; an existence of soft and eternal peace. [2:135]

No one lives a life of "soft and eternal peace," except in deluded dreams, and Crane knew it. "He was almost illusion-less," Berryman said of Crane, "whether about his subjects or himself. Perhaps his only illusion was the heroic one; and not even this . . . escaped his irony."

*Society everywhere is in conspiracy against
the manhood of every one of its members.
Society is a joint-stock company, in which
the members agree, for the better securing
of his bread to each shareholder, to surrender
the liberty and culture of the eater. The
virtue in most request is conformity. Self-
reliance is its aversion. It loves not realities
and creators, but names and customs. Whoso
would be a man, must be a non-conformist.*

EMERSON, "Self-Reliance"

Chapter Three

The Individual, Society, and Chaos: Other Genres and the Epic Stance

The self-reliance upon which *The Red Badge* places such high value is not so much transcendental as pre-Christian or even Homeric. Related to *areté*, Crane's sense of self-reliance evokes tasks and accomplishments which in the end are fulfilled largely through one's own abilities. Nevertheless, like Emerson's, Crane's self-reliance strives for "realities." Except for *The Red Badge*, none of Crane's works places in a formally epic frame the task of seeing reality without the filters of individual imagination or group security. There may be three reasons for this. First, as Crane said, "I have used myself up in the accursed *Red Badge*";[1] that is, while he had the patience and staying power to do it once, Crane was also a young man in a hurry. Second, having gained the confidence to write at length about epic themes in his war novel, Crane could now convey those themes without formal epic trappings. And finally, within the epic he found genres which allowed him to carry the theme in concert with his talent for writing short fiction.

The epic is the only classical genre to encompass tragedy and comedy. Comedy fit Crane's genius for parody, and tragedy became the mainstay of his best fiction after *The Red Badge*. Tragedy in particular is so bound up with epic that Crane could easily blend epic and tragic structures. Aristotle felt that while differences existed between tragedy and epic, there were also important similarities. Both, for example, are imitative, dramatic, concerned with universal truths, and contain *peripeteia* ("reversal"), *anagnorisis* ("recognition"), and great suffering. Indeed, for Aristotle the most significant difference between epic and tragedy is length.[2]

Crane often fuses tragedy and epic by emphasizing one of their more significant shared qualities: heroic effort. Dr. Trescott in *The Monster*, the Swede in "The Blue Hotel," the men in "The Open Boat" all engage in heroic tasks within a context of tragedy and a theme of epic. Even a great comic story like "The Bride Comes to Yellow Sky" has its tragic significance in the futile efforts of Scratchy Wilson against the juggernaut of eastern "civilization" and an epic significance in the universal truth implied by the American "showdown."

Early in his career, in *Maggie, a Girl of the Streets*, Crane attempted to blend myth and tragedy with his naturalism, but without incorporating epic. Partly as a result, *Maggie* is somewhat muddled and angry and lacks some of the scope of those works which incorporate epic. It nevertheless demonstrates that very early in his career Crane was able both to draw from classical sources and to sustain them in longer fiction, and, as Gullason shows, that tragedy helped shape that fiction.[3]

Maggie, a Girl of the Streets

Whatever else it may be, *Maggie* is Crane's first sustained attempt at putting together classical materials in a modern form. The novel is more than a paradigm of naturalism and more than the parody of the sentimental slum novel Eric Solomon suggests;[4] part of the naturalism of *Maggie* is the determinism of tragedy, and the significant parody focuses upon a displacement of classical myth—an inversion of the Persephone / Proserpina myth driven with such a nihilistic force that the normal conservative limits of parodic intention are set aside.

A "voracious reader" of the classics, Crane could have encountered the Persephone myth in many places, but most likely in Ovid. Ovid's account describes Proserpina, the virgin daughter of the harvest deity Ceres, as picking flowers in a woodland meadow-garden that surrounds a pool with eternal spring and sunshine. Suddenly, Dis, dread god of the underworld, comes through the pool driving a chariot. In a flash he sees, loves, rapes, and carries the hapless ex-virgin back through the pool to Hades. Missing her daughter, Ceres lays waste the land in a frenzy of fear and lamentation until informed of Proserpina's whereabouts. Ceres then races to Jove for arbitration. He finally decrees, according to one account, that Proserpina must henceforth divide her time between earth and hell.[5] In short, it is a season myth, a Greek and Roman pagan Genesis of death and rebirth.

Crane inverts this myth. Instead of Proserpina's hopeful, fecund, rural spring, Maggie's season is a despairing, sterile, urban "autumn [which] raise[s] yellow dust from cobbles and swirl[s] it against an hundred windows" (1:11). Maggie spends her childhood peering from corners into a "dark region" of "frantic quarrels" where cooking odors fill the "darkening chaos of backyards" with "smoke" and "steam" and the "hiss" of boiling potatoes (1:11–14). Full darkness ironically illuminates an even greater horror; for then, should the demon called "mother" awaken, "all the fiends would come from below" (1:19). Maggie's father says it outright: "Home reg'lar hell" (1:17).

Such as they were, childhood and adolescence end early. By the fifth chapter, the father and the "babe," Tommie, have died; brother Jimmie has grown up "hardened," and "the girl, Maggie, [has] blossomed in a mud puddle." Beauty, however, provides no way out, only the choice between the hells of the sweatshop and the street.

The possibility that Proserpina's pool is here turned into Maggie's mud puddle is less important to the myth's displacement than the fact that like Proserpina, Maggie is identified with flowers. Unlike Proserpina, Maggie spends all of her life in a sort of hell, and she is therefore associated with flowers in a way that inverts the original myth's intention. Instead of symbolizing the fecundity of life, flowers are associated with death.[6] Maggie's method and purpose in picking flowers, for example, contrast markedly with Proserpina's: Tommie "went away in an insignificant coffin, his small waxen hand clutching a flower that the girl, Maggie, had stolen from an Italian" (1:20).

When she first sees Pete, her eventual lover, Maggie looks at him as a flower might first view the sun. She initially becomes aware of his presence through "half-closed eyes" (1:25) which open like blooming flowers ultimately to behold a "golden sun" (1:35), a Sol, who departs from their first meeting in "a sort of blaze of glory" (1:27–28). Her natural feelings of inferiority before this sky-god are similarly conveyed through flower imagery. Before their first date, she finds "the almost faded flowers in the carpet-pattern" to be "newly hideous" (1:28). In an effort to make her home more presentable for him, she buys "flowered cretonne for a lambrequin" (1:28). Her mother gets drunk and tears the lambrequin, so that Pete arrives to find its "knot of blue ribbons" looking like "violated flowers" (1:29).

Emotionally and physically violated at home and in the factory, where she feels herself "shrivelling" (1:35) in the heat, Maggie increasingly looks towards Pete as a more natural source of warmth and as a way out of the burning hells of home and work. Knowing that "the bloom upon her cheeks" (1:35) will fade some day, she yearns to bask in the warmth of the sun.

Pete is opposite from what Maggie thinks he is. He is not Sol, but rather the Bowery equivalent of Dis. Part of Pete's "courtship" of Maggie, for example, the trip to the Museum of Arts, may be taken for a guided tour through Hades. Here Maggie wanders through "vaulted rooms" guarded by "watch dogs," while Pete describes a display of mummified remains: "Look at all dese little jugs! Hundred jugs in a row! Ten rows in a case an' 'bout a t'ousand cases!" (1:36). Even Dis is amazed that death has undone so many . Maggie's mother, Mary Johnson, identifies Pete in Christian terms when she throws Maggie out of the house: "Yeh've gone t' d' devil, Mag Johnson. . . . Go t'hell wid him, damn yeh, an' good riddance. Go t' hell an' see how yeh likes it" (1:41).

Maggie goes, and for a time she likes it. Pete is a bartender and a sort of Bowery king, for it is he who receives alms and dispenses oblivion. The palace of his kingdom is the bar, and here all his subjects, including Maggie, are treated to fine Saturday nights. The saloon is a liquid Circe's isle, a place, too, where sirens sing "seductively to passengers to enter and annihilate sorrow or create rage" (1:45). Those places Pete takes Maggie have a liquid, misty underwater effect, creating a near parody of classical hells. The bar is filled with jars of pickles "swimming in vinegar" and "many-hued decanters of liquor" (1:45). In another beer hall there is a moist "smoke cloud" that "eddie[s] and swirl[s] like a shadowy river" (1:57).

Outside the barrooms, Pete is still associated with Hades, particularly at crucial moments in his relationship with Maggie. After Mary packs them off "t' hell," Maggie asks Pete if he loves her. His reply: "O, hell, yes" (1:42). When he abandons her, he says, "Go to' hell" (1:67). Yet when he reflected upon this act, "he did not consider that he had ruined Maggie," or that "her soul would never smile again," just as Dis failed to dwell on whether Proserpina would be happy in Hades. In hell, "souls did not insist upon being happy."

From her brother Jimmie, to whom Maggie might expect to be able to turn, there is no help. He too is a little Bowery god, a lesser Pete, and is described as a perverted Phaethon or as one who could change the course of Sol. Jimmie is a truck driver who is convinced that "he and his team had the unalienable right to stand in the proper path of the sun chariot, and if they were so minded, obstruct its path or take a wheel off" (1:22). Thus, while Jimmie may not be the equal of a bartender like Pete, he is nevertheless a "god-driver" who wields "flame-colored fists" (1:23).

More important to *Maggie*'s connection with the Proserpina myth, however, is the identification of Jimmie with Jove. Sitting high on the seat of his truck he sees pedestrians as "pestering flies" might be viewed by wanton boys: "He continually stormed at them from his throne" (1:22). Moreover, Jimmie plays (or rather fails to play) Jove's role as arbitrator in the case of Maggie's seduction. Hearing that Maggie had gone to hell, "storm-clouds swept over his face" (1:42). He rushes out to fight with Pete, but after escaping from a policeman who breaks up the fight, Jimmie gives up: "Ah, what d' hell?" He later reconsiders, saying to his mother, "Maybe it 'ud be better if I fetched her home" (1:55). But Mary objects—she'll never git anodder chance dis side of hell" (1:56). Jimmie is a coward who will never get closer to Olympus than when he stood, a defiant infant, atop "a heap of gravel" and threw stones at "the howling urchins from Devil's Row" (1:7); for, unlike Jove, who manages a compromise, Jimmie gives in completely with his decision to "damn her" (1:56).

The fourth and most pernicious of the Bowery deities is Mary Johnson. She is a Yorkshire Ceres, a malignant, marauding sow of a woman, who eats her own farrow—a perfectly inverted Ceres. While Ceres engages in destruction when her daughter is kidnapped, she is almost always creative, as a fertility goddess should be. From first to last, Mary Johnson is destructive. At the beginning of the novel, when Maggie, Jimmie, and their father come into the room, a "large woman is rampant." She grasps Jimmie "by the neck and shoulder [and shakes] him until he [rattles]," her "massive shoulders" heaving and her "huge arms" flailing (1:12). Tossing Jimmie in a corner and placing "her immense hands on her hips," she turns towards her husband with a "chieftain-like stride" (1:13). A fight ensues; she wins; he leaves. An emotional gladiator, Mary howls, screams, and roars her way through the novel. Besides damning someone "t' hell" about two dozen times, Mary often whips herself into such drunken physical and emotional frenzies that she collapses screaming or snoring on the floor.

While Ceres does her best to save Proserpina from a hellish fate, Mary is largely responsible for causing Maggie's. Mary's response to her daughter's dating of Pete is one which drives Maggie away. When Maggie is making preparations for and awaiting her first date with Pete—presumably a special time for daughter and mother—Mary reacts with a vehemence that is unusual even for her: "[Maggie's] mother drank whiskey all Friday morning. With lurid face and tossing hair she cursed and destroyed furniture all Friday afternoon. When Maggie came home at half-past six her mother lay asleep amidst the wrecks of chairs and a table. Fragments of various household utensils were scattered about the floor" (1:29). Here, too, the lambrequin is singled out by Mary's wrath. Actions such as these, added to Mary's pointed "t' hell wid him an' you," combine to give Maggie little alternative but to take up with Pete. Between the efforts of Ceres and Jove, an at least partial redemption of Proserpina is effected. Between Mary and Jimmie, Maggie is irrevocably damned.

Finally, if Ceres represents part of a rigidly ordered cycle of seasons, Mary personifies the chaos that howls through a seasonless hell. She represents too the destructive rage that in Ceres is an ultimately creative expression of grief. In either case Mary inverts the creative passion of Ceres, makes it sterile, annihilating, and chaotic.

Still, Mary's vision of herself, like Jimmie's and Pete's, is opposite the reader's. She sees herself as a genuinely loving mother, but the expression of that vision is banal. After Maggie's death, mourners come to Mary, who then slobbers over Maggie's baby shoes—"I kin remember when she used to wear dem"—and lapses into delirium tremens of anguished self-indulgence: "Jimmie boy, go git yer sister an' we'll put d' boots on her feets!" (1:76). Like her other actions, Mary's final act mocks Ceres's wild but genuine sorrow.

At times, then, *Maggie* perfectly inverts the Proserpina myth. Mary is a Ceres who stands on her head; Pete is Dis mistaken for Sol, his heavenly opposite; Jimmie, hell's truck driver, is associated both with Phaethon and with Jove turned moral cripple. And Maggie is Proserpina deluded into thinking that Dis will deliver her to a higher, finer world, not a lower one. As Milne Holton perceptively suggests, "*Maggie* is in a sense a bipolar novel; at one polarity is illusion, at the other chaos."[7]

But Maggie only *seems* to move from a lower to a higher (even if illusory) and again to a lower world, the inverse of Proserpina's recurring seasonal journey within the boundaries of the myth. Assuming this, however, invites a further induction: if the Proserpina myth finally generates some hope, then *Maggie* must express hopelessness. And that injects an element of irony into parodic inversion. While irony's presence does not preclude the use of parody, it does destroy the neat quid pro quo displacement of the myth in the novel. *Maggie*'s hell is not Dantesque but classical; its circles rest on a plane that slopes almost imperceptibly downward, from, Gullason says, "misery to more misery."[8] Maggie moves from one circle to another, but not from a lower to a much higher world, for there are no significantly higher worlds. *Maggie*, then, not only inverts the Proserpina myth, but also flattens it. Hope is indeed a vacuous emotion.

The tragic structure of *Maggie* is based upon this myth. But tragedy is a genre of hope: the chaos unleased in tragedy is controlled again at the end. The typical classical tragedy follows this line: the hero, defined in part as paradoxically more than human and at the same time all too human, makes a mistake (*hamartia*) by wittingly or unwittingly violating some law of the gods or man, a law which, by the way, may be written or unwritten, just or not. Attempting either to pursue or reverse the course determined by his mistake, the hero must make choices. Personality, events, the makeup of either the material or the human world—all of which may or may not be divided into "fate" or "environment"—conspire so that he always makes the wrong choices. Each choice leaves him with fewer alternatives, until he is left with only two courses of action. Either produces ruin. If things go well in the beginning, a reversal occurs, usually near the middle of the tragedy, and soon thereafter a recognition of inevitable doom. Through it all, there is a sense that things are fated to happen, that the lives of men and women are determined.

Maggie's most particular "mistake" seems to be that of seeing Pete as a "golden sun." Her reversal of fortune occurs, as in epics, precisely in the center of the novel (chapter 10 of nineteen chapters) where it is reported indirectly and euphemistically that Maggie is a virgin no more. Holton also notices the structural bifurcation: "If we are to assert that central to Crane's concern is the representation of Maggie's and Jimmie's illusions then it is the causes of those illusions which are set forth in the first half of the book, their consequences in the second."[9] Maggie's recognition, typical of tragedy, comes soon afterward. In keeping with Crane's realism, however, Maggie's recognition comes slowly, dimly, and completely. At first, when Pete leaves her in a bar to go panting after another woman called "Nell," "Maggie [is] dazed.She could dimly perceive that something stupendous had happened" (1:60). Unable either to fully realize the significance or to comprehend the tragedy of her situation, she does not ask "What happened?" or "Why?" but rather "Who?" (1:67). In its dark moments, tragedy always asks this question. When it edges toward nihilism, as, say, in the Book of Job, tragedy fails to answer. *Maggie* fails to answer and takes a further step toward nihilism by making all gods illusory.

With such creatures as Mary, Jimmie, and Pete controlling her life, Maggie is quickly caught in a straightjacket of fate that slowly but inexorably squeezes the life out of free will. Her first choice is between work and prostitution, a choice between circles in a nearly horizontal hell. Her second is between work and Pete. The third between prostitution and suicide. The last seems to be between freezing to death on a street corner and committing suicide by jumping in the East River. She chooses the latter. A small act, perhaps, and probably not even an heroic one, but, at least, for once, she chooses to act. Finally, if Maggie seems to lack the quality of being "more than human" required of tragic protagonists, she has an abundance of the other half of the paradox—she is, quite clearly, "all too human."

But again, the nihilistic irony of the story twists the tragic structure. Maggie's biggest "mistake" is not so much in misperceiving Pete, but rather in being born. Her circumstances—her poverty, illiteracy, and gender—grip too tightly. It is impossible for Maggie to gain that world-defying, more than human strength of great tragic heroes. Death is from the very beginning the only way out; she cannot, after all, hitch up her skirts, stride up Fifth Avenue, and inherit a department store. There are no heroes in this world. By including the elements of tragedy in *Maggie*, but then refusing the protagonist full tragic stature, Crane mocks the genre; for tragedy, like epic, is a hollow form without greatness and heroism to fill it up.

Maggie also reverses tragedy because it lacks a final optimism. Tragedy is a positive genre; order *must* be restored in the end; life must look better for most people. All that is left at the end of *Maggie* is a black, howling, nihilistic vision. All that is left is chaos in the figure of Mary Johnson, screaming out an ironical forgiveness. Everything that happens in *Maggie* is destructive, self-annihilating, and darkly ironic. One can say of Oedipus, Lear, or Macbeth, "If only he had not defied the gods." But for Maggie there are no "if onlies." In Crane, as in Aristophanes, "Whirl is king, having deposed Zeus."

The Monster

Maggie and *The Monster* evoke a similar sense of classical, even tragic fate. J. C. Levenson, in one of his excellent introductions to the various volumes of the Virginia edition, describes Trescott's tragic dilemma as one in which "Trescott, firmly set in the established order and prompted only by motives of which his society approved, acted to bring on himself a relentless process of exclusion and alienation."[10] Like Maggie, Dr. Trescott is led down a road which gradually leaves behind all side trails until his only choice is essentially made for him by his circumstances. One difference between the two is that Trescott seems to have more choices. He is more intelligent and educated, and he is certainly more conscious of the consequences of his choices. Another difference is that while retaining a pattern of tragedy similar to *Maggie's*, *The Monster* draws from epic traditions rather than exclusively from mythic.

Like *The Red Badge*, *The Monster* is divided into twenty-four sections, has a two-part structure, includes flashbacks, and contains at least one epic simile—"The fire was already roaring like a winter wind among the pines" (7:21). On the other hand, the epic elements of *The Monster* are more muted than those of *The Red Badge*. It is as if Crane were now more confident of his materials and more able to convey an epic theme without relying so heavily upon epic trappings. The epic machinery so obvious in *The Red Badge*—*in medias res*, Homeric epithets and similes, the *deus ex machina*, Stygian streams—are all gone from *The Monster*. Similarly, the American history so pervasive in *The Red Badge*—the Civil War is everywhere, as well as the excruciatingly painful anatomy of a comparatively democratic army—while still important, becomes somewhat muted in *The Monster*. Relations between blacks and whites figure prominently, but perhaps even more encompassing is the burning of "Signing the Declaration" on Trescott's wall: independence and equality are as futile ideals for nations as for individuals. Indeed, Crane's notions about American history tend to reflect those about epic and history in general (the specifics of Crane's thoughts on American history may yet prove fertile ground for scholarly planting). Nevertheless, Crane's short novel of heroic effort in small-town America comes closer to reflecting Aristotle's "universal form" of epic than does *The Red Badge* because Crane can now eschew the many varied episodes required in the epical war novel.

Yet if *Maggie* is about the individual facing the chaos of the universe without the mediating power of a very settled and civilized group, *The Monster* demonstrates that occasionally one is forced into just as tragic a situation within a civilized society, in fact, because of that society. For Crane, small towns in America, like civilizations anywhere, exist in order to mediate between the individual and chaos. Ordered society blocks out reality and grants to the individual a sense of security, order, and intelligibility.

The Monster opens with a scene demonstrating that Dr. Trescott is a solid member of such a society. Like Wilson in the second half of *The Red Badge*, Trescott has been subsumed into the group and believes in its values. He demonstrates his belief in two ways in the opening chapter. First, when his young son, Jim, destroys a peony by driving his imaginary train over the flower garden, the elder Trescott punishes the boy mildly but firmly by banishing him from the garden. Commonly interpreted as a myth from Genesis or *Paradise Lost*, it may be viewed even more broadly. Crane's fictional children, from the occasional infant in "The Sullivan County Tales" to the child in "Death and the Child," are all representatives of a more "natural" universe. More or less civilized, or in the process of becoming so, they nevertheless visit upon ordered society enormous egos accompanied by wild imaginations that sometimes copy and often parody the imaginative mis-perceptions of their elders. Crane was fascinated by this aspect of children and used to watch them for hours in an attempt to get glimpses of the natural animal from them. The first scene of *The Monster* demonstrates what happens when civilization, fragile as a flower, is threatened by reality. Society cannot tolerate such intrusions. Flower gardens may be looked at as metaphors for society: both are imaginative manipulations of reality, fictions created out of chaos. So, too, the suburban lawn. While Jim is destroying the order of the garden, Dr. Trescott is controlling a slightly larger world by mowing his grass. So important is the mowing-of-lawn that in American society even today one's social standing may in part be deter-mined by how well this ritual is performed. Trescott's social standing must be very high indeed: "The doctor was shaving this lawn as if it were a priest's chin" (7:9).

The theme of *The Monster* is heroically tragic, a cognate of *Antigone*. It is a tragedy of what happens when private ethics conflict with public order. Antigone had to choose between obeying the private morality of burying a relative and the public law which forbade that relative's burial. Trescott must choose between his private sense of honor, which demands that he care for a man who saved Jim, and public "law," which demands that that man either die or be put away.

The man in question is Henry Johnson, a black hostler who

works for the Trescotts, and whose face was eaten by acid and burned in a fire after he had saved young Jim from a fire. Like the ruined peony in the first chapter, Johnson comes to represent the intrusion of reality into the illusions of the community. Take the familiar face from man, the accustomed behavior, the veneer of civilization, and, as in *Maggie*, "whirl is king." Trescott faces that reality as much as any of Crane's other characters, but he fails at first to reckon with the task of forcing the community to face it as well. When he does, he consciously sets himself upon a collision course with that society. Unlike Henry Fleming, Trescott cannot win even a temporary victory. The community utterly defeats him.

Part of the structure is formally epic, for the first twelve of the book's twenty-four chapters show Trescott trying to "do the right thing" by Henry Johnson, and incidentally by himself and the community. That is, he wants it both ways. When this fails because Henry frightens people, Trescott reaches his ethical low point, exactly midway through the novel: he tries to hide Henry in the country (on the periphery of the community) among Henry's "own kind." This, too, fails. Alex Williams, the black man whom Trescott pays to keep Henry, finds himself and his family disintegrating from the effects of Henry's presence.

Once again, as in many other stories, the stove forms the nucleus of civilization, and, in this instance, of the family. When Henry first appears in the Williams home, six of the children make a "simultaneous plunge for a position behind the stove" (7:35). On another evening, when Alex went cautiously to check on Henry's room, his wife "stood in front of the stove, and her arms were spread out in the natural movement to protect all her sleeping ducklings" (7:44).

In the face of such panic and of the fact that he is avoided by his neighbors (7:42), Alex capitulates. He is saved from having to decide to give up his six dollars a week for keeping Henry by

Henry's escape into town. Once in town, Henry frightens children and adults. When he is finally apprehended, the community incarcerates him and demands that Trescott "do something." This, the inevitable result of Johnson's disfigurement, constitutes the reversal of Trescott's fortunes.

Many epics contain tragedy. By the end of the *Iliad*, Achilles has learned much but has little time to live; Odysseus's last piece of knowledge is one of yet another journey; Vasco da Gama dies midway through Camoens's epic; Adam and Eve are driven from the garden; the permanence of Henry Fleming's heroism is defeated by his own memory. Trescott's tragedy is complete by the *anagnorisis*, the "discovery" at the very end of the novel that he has lost. He cannot retain his moral and ethical stance toward Henry Johnson and remain within the community: his family will suffer too much. He cannot give in to the community without doing irrevocable damage to his own sense of honor. A classically tragic dilemma.

Interestingly, the *anagnorisis* is described in remarkably similar language to that of Henry Fleming's moment of heroism, where "his mind took mechanical and firm impressions" of the blades of grass. Arriving home after making a final defense of his position, Trescott finds his wife crying because no one in the community accepted an invitation to her Wednesday reception: "A low table had been drawn close to the stove, . . . [the table] was burdened with many small cups and plates of uncut tea-cake. . . . Glancing down at the cups, Trescott mechanically counted them. There were fifteen of them. . . . As he sat holding her head on his shoulder, Trescott found himself occasionally trying to count the cups. There were fifteen of them" (7:64–65).

The difference between Trescott's and Henry Fleming's "mechanical impressions" betrays important distinctions between *The Monster* and *The Red Badge*. Fleming sees natural objects, Trescott sees artificial ones, products of a group civilization. Fleming cut through civilization to reach a limited but clear perception of nature. Trescott sees both more and less. As he counts the cups carefully arranged near the stove, Trescott perceives that he cannot win against the group. He is trapped by position and family in the cave of restricted vision which groups impose upon their members. The small town throws up smoke as effectively as Fleming's regiment, but because Trescott is not involved in the catalytic environment of war, he has no hope of even a fleeting escape. He must live within the group and the group refuses to go on *seeing* Henry Johnson. Interesting also, and as significant with regard to Crane's development, is that the achievement of an impressionistic vision is epically heroic in *The Red Badge*, and tragically heroic in *The Monster*. A slight change of literary angle, the distinction between epical and tragic heroism may nevertheless indicate that impressionism was already becoming for Crane less of a salvation and more of a curse.

As a metaphor for chaos, the disfigured Johnson represents for Crane what his friend Conrad called "the horror" in *The Heart of Darkness*. Prior to his disfigurement, Johnson is a kind of American small-town version of Conrad's harlequin. Milder, better, more dignified than the harlequin, Johnson is nevertheless less restrained and more "natural" than his counterparts in the white community, an acceptable parody, as it were, of class. With his lavender trousers, his elaborate manners in courtship, and his overall demonstrative behavior "among his own kind," Johnson is a parody of the small-town black at the turn of the century, as are several others in the *Tales of Whilomville*, as well as in two recently found stories.[11] Johnson is tolerated only because he "behaves himself" in his relations with the dominant white society. Unlike Marlowe, who withdraws from society, however, Trescott is damned when society withdraws from him.

The tenuous relationship of this black man and white society is broken when he sloughs off the vestiges of civilized appearance and behavior.[12] Allowed to walk among the people of the community, Henry reminds those people of what they might be like were the veneer of civilization stripped away, if the artificially imposed rationality of their behavior were suddenly destroyed. Such reminders cannot be allowed. It is this that Trescott sees when he counts the fifteen cups. Trescott is damned if he does and if he doesn't.

Western Stories

Stephen Crane's western stories add a particularly American flavor to his epic theme of the individual against the group. Almost invariably the essence of the stories involves the conflict between an idea of a western and heroic individualism and the onslaught of eastern group values. The eastern civilization moving west is domestic, stereotypically feminine, and based upon the will of the majority. The inhospitable landscape of the West, epitomized by the storm raging over the space-lost bulb in "The Blue Hotel," demands that the values of the group be held supreme simply because the chaos of the universe is much more immediately observable in the West than in the sometimes soft and often forgiving climate of the East. The betterment of the group is often seen in terms of capital. The Palace Hotel exists to glean money from railroad passengers, and the citizens of War Post, in "Moonlight on the Snow," are concerned that the violence endemic to heroic societies will chase away monied speculators from back east. But always behind this concern for money is a sense that capital exists not only to make people rich, but also to enable them to further insulate themselves from reminders of chaos. Warm fires hold back the storms, streetlights hold back the darkness, and other products of group civilizations help create an artificial environment removed as far as possible from the real.

In contrast, the most pristine of Crane's western heroes are Homeric in their simplicity, their acceptance of violence as violence—they have no need to explain it away in communal dissipation of guilt—and their sense of honor. Scratchy Wilson, although outwardly tainted by his eastern clothes, is inwardly a "simple child of the earlier plains." Unlike any other townsman in the western tales, Scratchy cannot follow self-interest when to do so goes against his code of honor. He cannot shoot down an unarmed and married man even though not to do it means the end of his way of life. And the Swede, an eastern tailor who dresses himself in the image of the western hero, cannot sit idly by, like the Easterner and the others, saying nothing while a man cheats at cards. It is the Homeric simplicity of these characters' motives that partly accounts for "The Bride Comes to Yellow Sky" and "The Blue Hotel" being Crane's best western stories, as well as perhaps two of the best "westerns" ever written. They are great not only because they distill the "western," but also because any such distillation is made better by partaking of the epic tradition.

The Bride Comes to Yellow Sky

"The Bride Comes to Yellow Sky" is primarily about the fall of America's Old West as it occurs within the structure of a submyth called "the showdown."[13] An erstwhile outlaw, and relict of the West's heroic days, is drunk and on a rampage. Meanwhile the town marshal is returning home on a train, bringing with him his bride. When the old outlaw, Scratchy Wilson, comes face-to-face with Marshal Jack Potter, Wilson is on the verge of shooting until he discovers the marshal's new "condition." Scratchy backs down, leaving Potter and the

bride, law and order, and a new civilization as victors. However, there are other myths in "The Bride" which need to be
explored, for through these myths Crane universalizes his
story, making the fall of the American West symbolic of all
mythical falls from Troy to Yellow Sky.

The outlines of the Potter / Bride story are similar to the
myth of Paris and Helen. In both a man returns from a journey
bringing a "bride," both men avoid confrontations, and both
in doing so fail to live up to their positions in the community.
In "The Bride" and the *Iliad*, these actions precipitate a fall of
the old order of Yellow Sky and the civilization of Troy.

Such similarities could be coincidental, but Crane was "a
voracious reader . . . of the classics of Greece and Rome," and
"The Bride" is riddled with significant epic conventions. Two
of the characters, for example, are described within the formu-
la of the classical epithet. Jack Potter, besides being called "the
marshal," is Scratchy's "ancient antagonist," and also "the
bridegroom." Scratchy himself is variously referred to as "a
wonder," "a man in a maroon-colored shirt," "he of the
revolver," and "the man." His voice, too, is heroic and reminiscent of Achilles' thundering challenges which leave the
Trojans shaking in their armor: his "cries rang . . . in a volume
that seemed to have no relation to the ordinary vocal strength
of a man" (5:116–17). And finally, the classical connection is
firmly planted by a western version of an epic simile. Chal-
lenging Potter's house, Scratchy "fumed at it as the winter
wind attacks a prairie cabin in the North" (5:118).

Using classical myth and conventions to extend and deepen
meaning is not unusual for Crane, but in "The Bride" classical
myth and convention are used for more than merely broaden-
ing the story's scope. They play a vital part in a mock-epic
treatment of the myth of the American West. One of the
standard techniques of the mock-epic is to describe realistic,
mundane actions in epic language, or to build expectations

with epic language in order to deflate the realistic performance which follows. Section 2 of "The Bride," for instance, provides an epic biography for Scratchy Wilson, who "is drunk and has turned loose with both hands" (5:114). The reader and the newcomer in the saloon are assured that "there'll be some shootin'—some good shootin'," for Scratchy is "a wonder with a gun" (5:116). We are told that in his efforts to entice someone into battle, Scratchy will often shoot at a door, a dog, a window, a house, or anything else that reminds him (or us) of domestic existence. Section 3 describes Scratchy's more realistic performance; Scratchy fails to live up to the expectations provided by section 2. He misses the dog. He misses the piece of paper nailed to the barroom door. He even commits two cardinal sins among mythic antagonists: he has to reload periodically, and he fumbles and drops his revolver when facing his opponent. A gunfighter may be many dastardly things—mean, cruel, beady-eyed, and unwashed—but he may not be clumsy. And few legendary gunfighters reload their guns. It is all too mundane.

The difference between the expectations of section 2 and the performance in section 3 is one of the themes of Shakespeare's *Troilus and Cressida*, another antiepic drama: "that the will is infinite, and the execution confined; that the desire is boundless, and the act a slave to limit" (3. 2. 89–91).

The realistic description which follows certain classical conventions also serves to deflate the mythical. Immediately after Scratchy's "cries of ferocious challenge" comes this charming deflation: "His boots had red tops with gilded imprints, of the kind beloved of little sledding boys on the hillsides of New England" (5:117). After hurling more challenges, and after the epic simile describing them, Scratchy, "as necessity bade him . . . paused for breath or to reload" (5:118). When Wilson and Potter face each other there is in the language a dignity, an earnestness, even a high epic seriousness: the revolver "was aimed at the bridegroom's chest. There was a silence. . . . The two men faced each other. . . . He of the revolver smiled with a new and quiet ferocity" (5:118–19). Puzzled at finding the marshal unarmed,Scratchy then poses some very un-Homeric questions: "If you ain't got a gun, why ain't you got a gun? . . . Been to Sunday-school?" (5:119).

The difference between expectation and performance is the difference between myth and realism, between what we want and what we have, between what we want to see and what is, and "The Bride" uses this mock-epic technique to debase the showdown, its participants, and the myths of civilizations' falls.

Another way to explore Crane's use of classical myth is to compare "The Bride" with a different story about the fall of the mythical American West, preferably one without significant classical parallels and conventions, and one which therefore neither universalizes nor mocks the myth of the American West. Closely resembling "The Bride" in setting, plot, characterization, and portrayal of the end of the American West, O. Henry's "The Reformation of Calliope" is such a story.

Set in a small West Texas desert town during the 1880s, "The Reformation of Calliope" describes an aborted showdown between one drunken gunslinger—Calliope Catesby—and three lawmen: Sheriff Buck Patterson and two of his deputies.[14] Catesby shoots his way down the main street of Quicksand, firing at dogs, Mexicans, weathervanes, windows, and chickens (Scratchy shoots at dogs and windows; Crane's intelligent and judicious Mexicans light out early). Stopped by a barrage of bullets, Catesby fights his way to the railroad station, which provides a fortress from which he can defend himself. Undaunted, Patterson ("Son of P[o]tter"?) charges into the station, is grazed by Catesby's bullet, and is lying unconscious when Calliope's mother, just arrived on the train, walks in to greet her son. Thinking quickly, Calliope manages to pin on Patterson's badge before his mother gets inside. When he regains consciousness, Patterson, too, thinks quickly, for he almost immediately takes in the situation, and while going along with Catesby's ruse, nevertheless manages to secure the latter's promise to reform. Calliope reforms because he does not want to disappoint his mother. Although "The Bride" begins with a railroad and "The Reformation" ends with one, both are stories about a showdown which ends without death and without the "winner" winning. Calliope and Scratchy Wilson lose even though they have the drop on their opponents. They lose because the game changes; the game changes because a woman intervenes.

The stories' details, as Current-Garcia has noted, are also similar.[15] Both Scratchy and Calliope are "terrors," both have unnaturally loud voices (Scratchy's is epical; Calliope's earns him his name), both are inoffensive when sober. Scratchy "wouldn't hurt a fly—nicest fellow in town" (5:116); Calliope is "a quiet, amiable man" (5:302). Since both stories occur in desert towns, their sea imagery is incongruous. One of Scratchy's guns is called his "starboard revolver," and the bride is once described as "drowning" while standing on a dusty street. The "splenetic Calliope," on a similar street, "was steaming down the channel, cannonading on either side, when he suddenly became aware of breakers" (5:305). A final and very interesting detail concerns the personal "reformations" of Calliope and Scratchy. When he pins on Sheriff Patterson's badge, Calliope symbolically reforms. Scratchy Wilson performs no similar action in "The Bride," but he does say of the feud, "Well, I 'low it's off, Jack" (5:120). Later, as Holton and others have noted, in his only other appearance in Crane's fiction, Scratchy shows up wearing a badge as Potter's deputy in "Moonlight on the Snow." With these reformations, the "Old West" has fallen in both Yellow Sky and Quicksand.

The differences between "The Bride" and "The Reformation" are perhaps even more revealing than the similarities, particularly in the use of classical myths and conventions. The significance of the Paris / Helen myth is clear for "The Bride," but the epic parallels of "The Reformation" all have to do with a divine mother saving her son from disaster. Further, the Paris / Helen myth directly applies to the fall of civilizations, but the classical parallels in "The Reformation" do not. Third, the classical conventions of epithet and simile are effectively undercut by the detailed and realistic descriptions in "The Bride." The name "Calliope" is, of course, the same one given to the muse of epic poetry, but because there is no other indication of epic parallels in "The Reformation," there is no epic mockery of the myth of the American West.

Further, there is in "The Reformation" no sense of fate, ineluctable, inexorable, classical fate. Whatever potential "The Reformation" has for evoking a sense of fate is sacrificed to O. Henry's "trick ending." "The Bride," on the other hand, has this sense, for all things move toward the showdown.[16] Potter moves toward Yellow Sky in section 1; Yellow Sky's history, especially the clash between Wilson and Potter, is recounted in section 2, setting up the actual clash in section 4; section 3 describes Scratchy Wilson moving toward his destiny in front of the marshal's home. These movements are paralleled in a larger sense as well, and are epitomized in the description of the collision courses of the train and the river: "To the left, miles down a long purple slope, was a little ribbon of mist where moved the keening Rio Grande. The train was approaching it at an angle, and the apex was Yellow Sky" (5:111).

Another aspect of the difference between the scopes or relative universalities of the two stories lies in their opening lines. "The Reformation" is clearly, and quite broadly, a parody of Hamlet's speech to Guildenstern (2:2). In spite of Calliope's association with the universal and tragic emotions of the Dane, however, none of Hamlet's greatness rubs off on Catesby:

Calliope Catesby was in his humours again. Ennui was upon him. This goodly promontory, the earth—particularly that portion of it known as Quicksand—was to him no more than a pestilent congregation of vapours. Overtaken by the megrims, the philosopher may seek relief in soliloquy; my lady find solace in tears; the flaccid Easterner scold at the millinery bills of his women folk. . . . Calliope, especially, was wont to express his ennui according to his lights. [P. 301]

The attempt at largeness here is through a comparison of Calliope to the microcosm of people regarding their relative reactions to depression. The effect is comic and is intended to be. The effect of "The Bride's" opening paragraph, on the other hand, is macrocosmic; there is a sense of epic sweep and of a movement toward some destiny:

The great Pullman was whirling onward with such dignity of motion that a glance from the window seemed simply to prove that the plains of Texas were pouring eastward. Vast flats of green grass, dull-hued space of mesquite and cactus, little groups of frame houses, woods of light and tender trees, all were sweeping into the east, sweeping over the horizon, a precipice. [5:109]

"The Bride," then, is similar to "The Reformation" in that both recount the fall of the Old West through the myth of the showdown. They differ in that the classical myths and conventions of "The Bride" are used to universalize the fall of the Old West and to mock the myths that tell the story of all such falls.

The danger inherent in using classical myth and convention to mock anything is that something epical may rub off on the thing being mocked. That such is the case in "The Bride" accounts for the sense of loss and pity over the end of an age and that age's heroes. One feels it for Hector and Troy, and, to a lesser degree, for Scratchy Wilson and Yellow Sky. One even feels it for the bartender's dog, who, though accustomed to being "kicked on occasion," is described in words usually reserved for the horse, the most common and yet noble of epic animals. When Scratchy shot at him, the dog "walked diagonally," "broke into a gallop," "screamed," "wheel[ed]," and "flurried" (5:117). Certainly, the dog mocks the noble horse, but the dog also gains a little of the horse's dignity from the description. The same is true, especially at the very end, of Scratchy Wilson. In spite of the comedy, there is something Homeric about the description of Scratchy in "The Bride's" last paragraph: "'Married!' He was nòt a student of chivalry; it was merely that in the presence of this foreign condition he was a simple child of the earlier plains. He picked up his starboard revolver, and . . . he went away. His feet made funnel-shaped tracks in the heavy sand" (5:120).

This old and simple warrior of the windy plains of Yellow Sky has been defeated and is sailing home, funnel-shaped wakes whirling briefly from his port and starboard boots. Like an old landed sailor, Scratchy is out of his element, his guns as incongruous as oars scratching across the sand of western Texas.

The Blue Hotel
"The Blue Hotel" is the winter of Yellow Sky's summer discontent. The two are companion stories, representing the classically tragic and comic faces of the same theme: the failure of the western myth. Some of the characters in "The Bride" are nearly reproduced in "The Blue Hotel." The Easterner, Mr. Blanc, comes west and aids in the murder of the western myth revived or recreated by the Swede. Although a Westerner, Jack Potter travels west to Yellow Sky from San Antonio, only to confront and defeat the western myth preserved by

Scratchy Wilson. A fundamental difference between the two stories, however, is the disparity between their genres: Scratchy's fall tends to be comic; the death of the Swede, on the other hand, is formally tragic.[17]

"The Blue Hotel" has long been recognized as tonally tragic,[18] and the Swede variously interpreted. At best, like the story, he appears as a pathetic, deluded (if not insane) bundle of naturalistic humors. The Swede is none of these, but rather is a rare example in American literature of the formal "high" tragic figure first flourishing in Greece and last in the late Renaissance. The kings, queens, and jacks that lie helplessly on the floor of the Palace Hotel have a classical significance not only by contrast to the commoners of the American prairie, but in comparison with them as well. And if other characters strike one as run-of-the-mill people, then the Swede stands out from them like a colossus bestriding the narrow Nebraska town of Fort Romper much as Caesar straddled the Mediterranean from Rome to Egypt. One reason is that the Swede is the center of a scenario of high tragedy; another is that he alone of the characters embodies Crane's personal definition of the heroic: that a man be "merely responsible for his quality of personal honesty."[19]

To be sure, the Swede's vision is false, but he does not know it until the moment of his death, and it is more important to tragedy that he remains true to that vision. The Swede sees the world as a place that still holds out the possibility for individual heroism, honesty, and truth. He stakes his life on it and he fails because the world (the West) does not live up to that vision. Nevertheless, there may be "something in the failure," and that something is the stuff of high tragedy.

Crane's naturalism and pessimistic determinism apply equally to "The Blue Hotel" and to any of a number of Renaissance high tragedies. "The Blue Hotel" employs as sophisticated and formalistic a sense of classical fate as does, say,

Chapman's formal high tragedy *Bussy D'Ambois* or *King Lear*, which Crane apparently knew.[20]

As tragic heroes, Bussy D'Ambois and the Swede have much in common. "I am for honest actions," says Bussy, and he comes into the court of Henri III of France to prove it. In Chapman's analysis, the court is full of deceit and dishonesty, a place where "moral virtues" become "disfigured with the attires of men" (1. 2. 47–48). Naturally, as any man who acts and speaks with complete honesty in the world, Bussy makes enemies. He also makes the honest mistake of succumbing to the very real desires of another man's wife. The combination of the two, both of which arise from the single source of his brave adherence to his vision of "honest actions," causes his death. Nevertheless, despite frailties and misconceptions, he is to the other characters as Hercules is to other mortals, a point reinforced by some dozen allusions to Hercules throughout the drama.

Like Bussy, the Swede is great largely because he is an honest man in a dishonest world, "a fool," in Swift's words, "among knaves." He is great because he is willing to act upon his concept of what is true and honest in a world of deceit and deception. He is great, even heroic, because, unlike the mass of men, he is willing to dare, even to defy, the fates, and consequently to rise even as he falls. A writer's concept of the heroic may or may not be conventional (certainly, with Crane it is not), but if the tragic protagonist is elevated to tragic stature, it is because he has remained true to his creator's conception of what it takes to be heroic, to be a giant among men.

The Swede is also a "foreigner" who thrusts himself into an unfamiliar and hostile world. After arriving at Fort Romper, Nebraska, by train in the middle of a blizzard, this "shaky and quick-eyed Swede" is enticed, with two other men, to stay at the Palace Hotel by Pat Scully, the hotel's owner-manager.

When they reach the hotel, they discover that, besides the Swede and Scully, there are also Scully's grown son, Johnnie, a "tall cowboy," a "silent little man from the East," and a farmer.

The world inside the blue hotel reverberates with classical echoes, as do many high tragedies, but "The Blue Hotel" particularly focuses on allusions to a plethora of Homeric conventions. Most of these conventions appear in the language of the narrator and function to raise the tragedy from the commonplace to the heroic: "Among the conventions of epic diction we find the patronymic, 'John, son of Scully,'; the stock epithet of the farmer with 'whiskers both gray and sandy,' 'of both gray and sandy whiskers'; the studied and solemn anaphora, 'One was a . . . Swede; one was a cowboy; . . . one was a . . . man from the East,' and the triple 'What do I keep?' of the outraged hotel proprietor; understatement, 'He [the terrified Swede] resembled a badly frightened man.'" Weinig also finds that Homeric conventions apply both to setting and to action, including "challenges to group engagement (the card games)" and to "single combat (resolution by ordeal of the argument over Johnnie's cheating)." The Homeric setting appears in the social structure in "the patriarchal household whose daughters minister to guests in Homeric simplicity and whose ceremonious hospitality (complete with ritual ablution) brooks no violation."[21]

Although "The Blue Hotel," like *Bussy D'Ambois*, is complete with classical parallels, the Swede, unlike Bussy, does not arrive fully formed as a hero. He does not begin as a brash and saucy fellow. But it is characteristic of most, if not all, of Crane's heroes, like the heroes of nearly all American writers, that heroism consists in discovering what it is to be a hero and then acting upon that discovery. Perhaps this is because American writers, lacking the traditions of Europe, must first create their heroes and force them through the process of becoming heroes before turning them loose on the world. Interestingly, the process is not peculiar to America, for it is also closely followed in such ancient epics as the *Aeneid*. The first part of "The Blue Hotel" creates the Swede as a hero who perceives something to be true and who grows until he is able to act honestly and openly upon his perception.

The central human action of the first scene within "the portals of the blue hotel" is a card game played beside the stove (the center of civilization in the hotel): "Scully's son Johnnie was playing High-Five with an old farmer. . . . They were quarreling" (5:143). The "quick-eyed" Swede cannot be assumed to have missed any of this quarrel, or even the reason for the quarrel. If the Swede saw Johnnie cheating, and he believes himself to be in the "Old West," where card games traditionally end with cheating exposed and murder imposed, then his resembling "a badly frightened man" is both explicable and understandable. That the Swede read dime novels explains his "unexplainable excitement" as he watches a second card game between Johnnie and the farmer. The pattern becomes obvious when "the play of Johnnie and the graybeard was suddenly ended by another quarrel. The old man arose while casting a look of heated scorn at his adversary. He slowly buttoned his coat, and then stalked with fabulous dignity from the room" (5:145).

Unable to contain himself any longer, "in the discreet silence of the other men, the Swede laughed" (5:145). A metaphor for the story, this statement also emphasizes that the Swede knows, as the others should, that Johnnie has been cheating. The others probably know it, too, but they choose to ignore it in the interest on their own safety and to concentrate on the Swede: "Men by this time had begun to look at him askance, as if they wished to inquire what ailed him" (5:145).

A third game is "formed jocosely" with the cowboy and Johnnie becoming partners, while the Swede and the Easterner pair up. The Swede is frightened ("He strode toward the men . . . as if he expected to be assaulted"), but he plays. His instinct for engaging the enemy overcomes his instinct for survival when, after the "board whacking" cowboy and Johnnie continually throw down "aces and kings," he suddenly addresses Johnnie with a barely disguised accusation of cheating: "I suppose there have been a good many men killed in this room" (5:146). This rather subtle yet brave or foolhardy remark, given the Swede's notions about card games played in the West, amounts to an accusation, but it is couched in language from a context that the others do not yet understand or admit.

The cowboy wants to know what is going on and Johnnie replies that he does not know what the Swede is talking about. When the Swede appeals to his "partner," the Easterner, he gets no help; Mr. Blanc replies, "after prolonged and cautious reflection, 'I don't understand you'" (5:146). Here are revealed two motives. First, that "cautious reflection" of the Easterner clearly implies that he knows Johnnie is cheating, but chooses to say nothing. At the end of the story, the Easterner admits to the cowboy that he knew Johnnie was cheating. Second, the Swede now has reason to believe that there is a conspiracy against him: "Oh, I see you are all against me. I see—" (5:146). The cowboy next brings matters to a head, or tries to: "'Say, what are you gittin' at hey?'" In response, "the Swede sprang up with the celerity of a man escaping from a snake on the floor. 'I don't want to fight,' he shouted" (5:146). Bussy speaks more about the Swede at this stage of the latter's development than about himself when he says: "I am for honest actions, not for great" (1. 1. 128). But the Swede soon realizes what Bussy discovers: there is little difference between "honest actions" and "great" ones. In this world of dishonesty, where power and even survival depend upon duplicity and conspiracy, only a great man, a heroic man, can maintain uncompromising honesty in his actions.

For the time being, however, the Swede attempts to have it both ways. He wants to expose the dishonesty of the place and still escape with his life. At this point, he has not stunned the others with the accusation of cheating; he has not brought it out in the open, and that is what is required when other people choose to be blind. Although the Swede wisely attempts to leave because he does not want "to be killed," the fates conspire against him in the person of Scully, who plays the classic role of the seducer. In the beginning, the hotel owner works "his seductions upon any man that he might see wavering, gripsack in hand" (5:142). Scully's hotel is a "court," for, as Weinig has shown, it closely resembles the social structure of Homeric palaces.

The reversal in the tragedy of "The Blue Hotel" is caused by Scully and changes the Swede into a doomed heroic figure. Scully follows the Swede upstairs and tries to dissuade him from leaving the hotel by showing him pictures of his two "departed" children, one dead, the other a lawyer in Lincoln. Unsuccessful, Scully next makes his final bid for the Swede's confidence by nearly forcing him to drink from the old man's private stock of whiskey. The Swede drinks, but does not accept the proffered initiation into the group:[22] the Swede "grabbed the bottle, put it to his mouth, and as his lips curled absurdly around the opening and his throat worked, he kept his glance burning with hatred upon the old man's face" (5:151).

Although the drink can be seen as an attempt at initiation, it could also be a challenge. The Swede thinks it a challenge, because he is now a changed man. The Swede, by accepting the drink, has decided to see things through. In very short order, the Swede rises in the society of the hotel by gaining both social and physical primacy over each of the main characters, one by one. He begins with a general dominance and then competes with individuals:

At six-o'clock supper, the Swede fizzed like a firewheel. . . . The Swede dominated the whole feast, and he gave it the appearance of a cruel bacchanal. He seemed to have grown suddenly taller; he gazed, brutally and disdainful, into every face. His voice rang through the room. Once when he jabbed out harpoon-fashion with his fork to pinion a biscuit the weapon nearly impaled the hand of the Easterner which had been stretched quietly out for the same biscuit. [5:154]

After disposing of the Easterner, the Swede goes after Scully's role as the "bacchanal's" host. Dominating the meal, the Swede attacks Scully as an individual by thumping the old man on his shoulder, which is still sensitive from an old injury. Then, the Swede insists on another game of "High-Five" over the objections of Scully, who had "gently deprecated the plan at first, but the Swede turned a wolfish glare upon him. The old man subsided" (5:155). Next, the Swede challenges Johnnie: "The Swede turned menacingly upon Johnnie. For a moment their glances crossed like blades, and then Johnnie smiled and said: 'Yes, I'll play'" (5:155). The Swede then dominates the card game by usurping the cowboy's role as "board whacker." Finally, the Swede forces the issue. Unable to play by the "rules" of the society, the Swede calls that society to task by going after Johnnie the only way that he can—with "three terrible words: 'You are cheating!'" (5:156).

A fight ensues during a storm and the Swede wins, despite the society's united support for Johnnie. His primacy is complete; the Swede has gained the summit. He has imposed his will and his vision of honesty on every man in the group, and they hate him for it. Finally, the metaphorical quality of "High-Five" becomes clear; these five men—Scully, Johnnie, the cowboy, Mr. Blanc, and the Swede—are representatives of humanity on any level from commoners on the American prairie to kings in some Homeric or French court. The Swede, with his "quality of personal honesty," rises to the heights. As a result, however, his splendor remains a "splendor of isola- tion" (5:161). The Swede is the only man capable of asserting his will enough to oppose the conspiracy of dishonesty in the hotel. It is a lonely position. Finally, such an act is as heroic in Nebraska as it is in the courts of kings, and there is no room on the tragic mountaintop for more than one.

The Swede has succeeded in reviving a tradition as old as Homer and as young as the "Old West." The problem is that this revival cannot be imposed on the West, let alone the whole world. The Old West simply no longer exists. The Swede, filled with a sense "of conquering and elate human- ity," oversteps the bounds of the blue hotel, marches into the storm, and finds a saloon where things are even more "East- ernized," where the participants are businessmen and gamb- lers with families. Here his attempt to assert an heroic domina- tion is cut off, as Bussy's was cut off. The Swede is killed. But with his death comes a recognition of fragile mortality. This individual man, "this citadel of virtue, wisdom, power, [is] pierced as easily as if it had been a melon" (5:168–69). Bussy provides meaning for the Swede's last wailing "cry of supreme astonishment" when, fatally wounded himself, he says: "Is my body then / But penetrable flesh?" (5. 3. 125–26).

For Chapman, for Crane, and for us, the only kind of high tragedy possible is based upon illusion. No hero can possess the mythic proportions required to keep whole nations and peoples secure under the brow of an eagle-eyed prowess. He can only imagine such a world, and then, for a brief moment, fulfill the requirements of that vision before falling victim to lesser men and to the "coward fates."

The story's end resembles a choric epilogue in Greek

tragedy.[23] In the final section, the Easterner, the most "Eastern" of the characters, speaks that epilogue when he says: "We're all in it" (5:170), echoing the epilogue of *Bussy D'Ambois*: "With many hands have you seen D'Ambois slain." But where *Bussy* acknowledges the aid of coward fates, the Easterner makes no such assertion, nor is it necessary that he should, since the story does. The Swede counts cadence for his own quick march down to doom. The cash register totals the amount of the Swede's sale while the other human agents watch and judge from the reviewing stand. To some extent the Swede is possessed by something inhuman and inexorable; a drummer boy for the Fates, he alone hears their tune. But if the society of "The Blue Hotel" does not live up to the Swede's heroic vision, then neither do the Fates, who, like the men in the hotel, are cowards.

Because surrounded by mean men and coward fates, the Swede must create an heroic stature through his own strength of will. He must surround his own mortal nature with heroic actions and he must impose those acts upon society. This is his glory and his curse, the cause of his rise and fall, his life and death. Because he is what he is, he must force himself to become like those "colossic statues, / Which, with heroic forms without o'erspread, / Within are nought but mortar, flint, and lead" (1. 1. 15–17).

The result of the conspiracy in "The Blue Hotel," however, goes beyond the death of that childlike but heroic innocence of the West which the Swede represents. In the dream or myth of an individual-centered world, a man can act and act heroically. If the Swede seems cowardly at times, it is because he, like Scratchy Wilson, with his maroon-colored shirt and sledding boots, has been tainted by the East. The Swede was, after all, a tailor, trained to create illusions around other men. With the coming of "ilictric street cars," as with the coming of the railroad, the heroic western society of individuals was doomed to be replaced. In Romper it had already been replaced by a group-oriented society. Part of the Swede's tragedy is that he raveled up the sleeve of a society that no longer existed. He created a tailor-made world for himself and imposed it on a group that, as it happened, was threatened by individualists. The end was inevitable. In America, it still seems to be inevitable; but in America, unlike most other places, the dream of the individual given expression in this country by Jefferson, Emerson, Thoreau, and Crane refuses to fade away.

"The Blue Hotel" is a formal high tragedy containing conscious echoes of the Homeric and Golden Ages of Greece. On another level, the story depicts, as do *The Red Badge* and a number of other pieces, the clash between two major cultural influences on the mind of Western man: the conflict between the Homeric notion of the individual-centered universe and the Christian-Roman idea of the group-centered culture. The trappings of a Homeric culture are draped on the walls of Scully's hotel, but also present, as Cox has shown, is the pervading influence of the Christian-group culture, which, through the imagery, shows the Palace Hotel to be at one time a Christian heaven and at another a Christian hell. Not only in the hotel, but in a number of the characters as well, there are references and allusions to Patrick Scully both as God and as Satan. Scully is even allied to the Holy Ghost, whose presence is revealed to the inhabitants by a banging on the walls of the house described as a "spirit tapping." And Johnnie is the remaining third of the trinity, the Son.[24]

These two cultural notions in "The Blue Hotel" are part of the same pattern that shapes *The Red Badge*. In both works there is a fearful hero who perceives things a certain way and then grows into the role he has created for himself in his imagination. The Swede thinks he is in the "Old West," so he creates it; he thinks he is going to die, so he does. Henry Fleming eventually becomes a hero and, for a time, precisely the kind of hero he had envisioned; he seldom thinks directly about getting killed, and he is not killed. There is even a confrontation with the group culture's "hero" in both works. Henry confronts Wilson, while the Swede confronts a more sinister and complex symbol: Johnnie. If Johnnie is indeed the Son, then his fight with the Swede is even closer to the confrontation in *The Red Badge*.

The Swede, like Henry Fleming in *The Red Badge*, has a close affinity to Achilles in the *Iliad*. All three are strangers in a strange land. Like Achilles, the Swede does not want to be killed and says so. Each spends the initial phase of his story avoiding conflict, but nevertheless keeps a sharp eye on the action. Finally, after deciding to act, both win initial victories over their chief adversaries: Achilles defeats Hector and the Swede pummels Johnnie. Yet each is doomed to die at the hand of a smaller, weaker, less heroic figure than himself: Achilles is killed by Paris's arrow and the Swede by "a long blade in the hand of the gambler" (5:168). More important to the analogy, Achilles and the Swede both know they are doomed. Achilles was forewarned by an oracle; the Swede merely seems to know: "I know I won't get out of here alive" (5:147).

The analogy between Achilles and the Swede is less important as a strict parallel than as an illustration of one tragic type. Not only does Achilles follow this epic paradigm, but so do Bussy D'Ambois, Aeneas, Roland, and a host of others from Leonidas to Lincoln who belong, as Rosenberg suggests somewhat redundantly, to "the epic of defeat."[25]

At any rate, it would seem that two worlds coexist in the Palace Hotel: the old and the new, the Homeric and the Christian, the West and the East. Both worlds are illusory in Scully's Palace. The old Irishman does not live up to his role as Homeric host, which would require that he stop the games. None of the guests expresses the ideal of Christian charity. The

Swede, simultaneously the most and least perceptive occu-
pant of this little world, creates a world that has long gone over
the horizon. The Wild West was dead before he got there, and
the sham world that takes its place will not brook the presence
of an individualist, or of a man who insists on playing games
by old rules.

If the Swede is a victim of his own false perceptions, then so
are the others, although they have a different vision. Around
this tightly knit little mob of placid "Easterners," the universe
is exploding. The storm exists for all men regardless of
"classes, creeds, egotisms" (5:142). The difference between
the old world of the Swede and the new world of the group is
that in the latter, where no one can be an individual, break the
rules, or "stand up and be a man," there is neither courage nor
hope. With the coming of streetcars and electric lights and
factories and the rest, the real darkness sets in, and men do
become "lice . . . caused to cling to a whirling, fire-smote,
ice-locked, disease-stricken, space-lost bulb" (5:165). For while
"conceit" is still "the very engine of life" (5:165), that egotism
has been transferred from the individual to the group, and the
old world has succumbed to the new as the eagle has given
way to the crows.

The irony of "The Blue Hotel" is that there can be no new
tragedy in this new world. The Swede, alone, must create or
recreate the old world in order to gain the stature of a tragic
figure, and he is killed for his trouble. The Easterner nearly
comes to a realization of tragic proportion at the end; that is, he
almost becomes an individual when he tells the cowboy in the
epilogue: "Johnnie was cheating. I saw him. I know it. I saw
him. And I refused to stand up and be a man" (5:170). But then
he loses it; he falls back into a group context in which his
individual conscience is assuaged in a bath of collective guilt. It
is also possible that the Easterner knows precisely what he is
doing, because his description of the guilt of the group widens

to include "from a dozen to forty women," and then narrows again, although not enough: "but in this case it seems to be only five men—you, I, Johnnie, old Scully, and that fool of an unfortunate gambler" (5:170). Although what he says is true, the Easterner fails, as he must, to remain true to that glimmer of "personal honesty" which, for Crane, may be translated, "to stand up and be man."

For Crane, the dream of the American West, indeed, of the idea of the "West" itself, was over. He had awakened to the reality that gamblers have families and that the vision of the individual had succumbed to the gospel of wealth. Such a vision sees the West as a place that must be made safe for capital and curbstones. The vision of limitless possibilities for profit replaces the dream of endless qualitative potentiality for the individual. The Swede's dream killed him because it came in the right place at the wrong time. He could impose his dream in the world of the hotel because, as MacLean suggests, there is "the world of 'what might be,' isolated, mysterious, highly symbolic." The saloon, on the other hand, "represents the world of 'what is,' at the heart of society, realistic, all but non-symbolic, and essentially amoral."[26] It is Crane's world, and ours.

Lesser Westerns

Some of the western stories fail to reach the greatness of "The Bride" and "The Blue Hotel" partly because the protagonists of the lesser stories often reflect Crane's own cynicism about the easternization of the American West. Instead of allowing classical forms and certain universalizing epical descriptions to evoke a sense of loss, Crane allows the editorializing comments of his protagonists to overpower both form and description.

In "Twelve O'Clock," a story about senseless killing, the conflict between western and eastern values is placed explicit-

ly in terms of anarchistic individualism versus group morality.
As one proponent of "eastern capiterlism" puts it, "Them rich
fellers, they don't make no bad breaks with their money. . . . I
tell you, one puncher racin' his cow-pony hell-bent-fer-
election down Main Street an' yellin' an' shootin' an' nothin' at
all about it, would scare away a whole herd of capiterlists. An'
it ain't right. It oughter be stopped" (5:172). And the way to
"stop it" is to eschew individualism in favor of collectivism:
"Organize: that's the only way to make these fellers lay
down."

Occasionally, however, a story only just misses greatness.
"Moonlight on the Snow," while not so good as Crane's best,
is nevertheless nearly as good as *Huckleberry Finn*'s Colonel
Sherburne episode, a story that resembles Crane's. As in "The
Bride," the showdown between the heroic protagonist and the
eastern values stirring in the townspeople never comes off:
because a woman intervenes, Tom Larpent is not hanged.
"Moonlight" is unlike "The Bride," however, because unlike
Scratchy Wilson, Larpent provides a running commentary on
the essential cowardice and greed of the group.

Larpent, a gambler who "had been educated somewhere"
(5:180), shoots a man for accusing him of cheating at cards and
for being, as Larpent says, "officious. Not enough men are
shot on that account" (5:183). The townspeople decide that
Larpent should be hanged because, as he again says, "the
value of human life has to be established before there can be
theatres, water-works, street cars, women and babies" (5:180).
Unlike the townsmen of Yellow Sky and Fort Romper, the
citizens of War Post are less sophisticated than the protagonist
who holds Homeric values. For them civilization is purely a
matter of economics: "'It's all well enough to set 'round takin'
money from innercent cowpunchers a'long's ther's nothin'
better; but when these here speculators come 'long flashin'
rolls as big as water-buckets, it's up to us to whirl in an' git

some of it.' This became the view of the town, and since the main stipulation was virtue, War Post resolved to become virtuous" (5:180).

While Larpent seems to hold values similar to Scratchy's and those assumed by the Swede, he is also so sophisticated that he may be suspected of being as "eastern" as he is "western." Not only educated, Larpent is also an entrepreneur—his "gambling house was the biggest institution in War Post." He "imports" his rye whiskey "secretly" from the East, reads Walter Scott, and assents to the resolution to hang anyone who kills anyone else.

A very complicated and outwardly civilized man, Larpent is fit to be Crane's mouthpiece in the familiar pillorying of clergymen and bartenders. The narrative introduces Mister Simpson as being "on occasion, the voice of the town. Somewhere in his past he had been a Baptist preacher. He had fallen far, very far, and the only remnant of his former dignity was a fatal facility of speech when half drunk" (5:183). Croaking "like a frog," Simpson is halfway through asking Larpent to admit to the killing when Larpent interrupts with his comment about shooting "officious" men: "As one fitted in every way by nature to be consummately officious, I hope you will agree, Mr. Simpson." The town's other leader, bartender Bobbie Hether, is treated to a similar scolding as Larpent is being led to the hanging: "I am resolved to devote my inquiries as to the welfare of my friends. Now, you, for instance, my dear Bobbie, present to-day the lamentable appearance of a rattlesnake that has been four times killed and then left to rot in the sun" (5:184).

Larpent is temporarily whisked away from the gallows by the agency that would be rid of him. A stagecoach arrives containing an eastern family, consisting of "a beautiful young lady," "two little girls," and "a white-haired old gentleman with a venerable and peaceful face": "The leather-faced men of

War Post had never imagined such perfection of feminine charm, such radiance; and, as the illumined eyes of the girl wandered doubtfully, fearfully, toward the man with the rope around his neck, a certain majority of the practiced ruffians tried to look as if they were having nothing to do with the proceedings" (5:185). The necktie party breaks up, leaving Larpent to sit on the steps with the rope around his neck. That evening he is permanently saved from the gallows by the same agency in the form of Jack Potter and his deputy Scratchy Wilson, who ride over from Yellow Sky to arrest Larpent for grand larceny, a charge brought by a tenderfoot, who, Larpent explains, could not play poker very well. Not only is he saved from hanging, but he will probably be freed since no one in War Post will testify against him. Here, everyone wins except the tenderfoot and the dead man, and the latter, at least, won't complain. Larpent will be free, and the community will gain the respectability it wants by bowing before the "reg-u-lerly cons-ti-tuted office of the law." War Post has engaged in an after-the-war skirmish; the outcome has already been decided in Yellow Sky and Fort Romper.

"Moonlight on the Snow" is a quintessentially American story filled with violence, broad humor, sarcasm, stupidity, pretentious respect for women, and hyperbole. But its wider implications fail to spread beyond those of the Christian myth. Larpent is, as the story says, "a devil," especially in the eyes of an eastern and Christian society. But Larpent is too jaded and the townsmen not individualized enough for the tragedy of the end of the heroic age in the West to have any force. And because it fails to partake of the epic tradition, it lacks the universalizing qualities that make "The Bride" and "The Blue Hotel" Crane's best western fiction.

Greece
Although Crane's best stories of the West owe their excellence

in part to their reliance upon classical antecedents, it is also true that he could occasionally and halfheartedly employ classical myths and epic trappings in some of his worst fiction. *Active Service*, Crane's only novel to rise from the ashes of his experiences as a correspondent during the Greco-Turkish War of 1897, may provide a sufficient case in point. Following an archetypically comic outline (chronologically this time not reversed as in "The Bride"), *Active Service* relates this story: boy and girl are in love, girl's parents (blocking figures) object, boy pursues girl and overcomes father's objections by rescuing the girl and her parents from danger and by manfully avoiding the snares of another woman.

More specifically, Rufus Coleman, Sunday editor of the *New York Eclipse*, is in love with Marjory, a daughter of a classics professor at Washurst University. Disapproving of the match on rather solid evidence that Coleman is "a gambler and a drunkard" (3:116), Professor Wainwright decides to include his daughter in a student tour of Greece, a tour the professor himself is to lead: "Separation! It is a cure that has the sanction of antiquity" (3:122). While touring ruins near Arta in Epirus, the group is trapped between the Greek and the Turkish lines. Meanwhile, back in the offices of the *Eclipse*, the not-so-mild-mannered reporter, Rufus Coleman, is discovering that he cannot do without Marjory. Arranging to become the *Eclipse*'s man in Greece, he heads for Europe and the front. Temporarily distracted between Ireland and England by a beautiful actress and dancer, Nora Black, Coleman finally arrives in Greece only to discover the plight of the Wainwright party. He jauntily sets out to rescue them and almost as jauntily does so. In fact, his rescue is effected by such apparent heroism, nobility, and aplomb, that the old professor is quite won over. Add dashes of "another woman" and a rich but base rival, both rather easily defeated (one of the book's many weaknesses), and the novel finishes like too many others with the hero and heroine about to kiss while the naiads sing. Specifically, with one notable exception during which Nora attempts to seduce Rufus, *Active Service* is even banally chaste, especially at the end, with Rufus telling Marjory "I haven't even kissed you yet—" (3:328), as they sit "in a secluded cove, in which the sea-maids once had played" (3:328).

Active Service is easily disparaged as a work of art. Stallman observes that "the prose is as starched as an 1890 collar-and-cuff, while structurally the novel is limp." Solomon calls it a parody of the love-adventure, and Levenson suggests that it was written solely for money while also exploiting a "yellow press conception of reality." Holton agrees and says that *Active Service* quickly becomes the very thing its first chapters parody.[27] It is difficult not to concur, especially since the promising classical allusions and parallels of the beginning soon fade away to relative insignificance.

The novel begins with a description of Professor Wainwright's study, a room presided over by a bust of Pericles, who presided as well over Greece's golden age by virtue of his persuasive powers and sagacity. Indeed, the entire room is visually suggestive of Mediterranean life: "The sunlight flowing through curtains of Turkey red fell sanguinely upon the bust of dead-eyed Pericles on the mantle" (3:113). Certainly, this is an accurate description of the famous and often-copied bust of Pericles, but "dead-eyed" is also reminiscent of the Matthew Arnold-Thomas Huxley debate over classical versus scientific education and of where Crane no doubt stood on the issue.[28] In such an instance, the implication would be that Wainwright is as blind to modern life as is the bust of Pericles. On the other hand, Pericles may be mentioned in order to provide a contrast between modern and ancient life to the detriment of the latter. In any case, Pericles provides a silent commentary upon the inability of Wainwright to bridge the gap between himself and his daughter and between the old and new generations.

Chapter 2 introduces Coke, Coleman's rich but essentially nasty and ineffectual rival for Marjory. Interestingly, Coke is introduced as part of an elaborate description of a mock-epic battle in which various classes of Washurst students are antagonists. Essentially harmless at first ("there were no blows"), there were nevertheless "phalanxes of shoulders" pushing forward and back. At this point the parodic situation becomes similar to the situation of the Trojan War, and Coke becomes a Paris figure insofar as he has broken a serious rule of conduct: he hits a freshman, and "a blow delivered openly and in hatred fractured a sharply defined rule of conduct" (3:120). No one in the Trojan camp is particularly happy about defending Paris from the Greeks, but they also know that since they have been attacked they cannot surrender Paris and Helen without doing violence to their sense of honor:

It was no longer a festival, a game; it was a riot. Coke, wild-eyed, pallid with fury, a ribbon of blood on his chin, swayed in the middle of the mob of his class-mates, comrades who waived the ethics of the blow under the circumstances of being obliged to stand against the scorn of the whole college as well as against the tremendous assaults of the Freshman. Shamed by their own man but knowing full well the right time and the wrong time for a palaver of regret and disavowel, this battalion struggled in the desperation of despair. [3:120]

After reading this, one cannot see *Active Service* as anything but parodic, for even at his worst Crane could not have written so ridiculous a redundancy as "desperation of despair" unconsciously. One of the problems with *Active Service* may indeed be its obviousness, as well as the fact that Crane does

not create antagonists even remotely worthy of the protagonist, who is himself not particularly worthy.

Chapter 3 introduces Coleman and is clearly a parody of
yellow journalism, but part of the force of the parody derives
from displacements of classical myths, or rather, of figures
from classical myth. The confrontation between Odysseus and
the Cyclops compares humorously with the meeting of the
small-town editor and the baby with "one-eye" and "semi-
human" parents. The "cow-eyed and yellow-faced" mother
compares unfavorably with cow-eyed Hera, who never ex-
ploited her children so grossly as does this mother.

The office of the *Eclipse* is first interestingly described, not by
a telling of what it looks like, but rather by telling what things
look like *from* it. The effect is the same as the description of the
countryside given through the eyes of the Little Man atop the
hill in "The Mesmeric Mountain," only here no specific pair of
eyes is identified. The effect is rather more Olympian than
mesmeric, the perceiving eyes more omniscient than those of
the Little Man; in short, the narrative point of view is faintly
reminiscent of Greek epic's occasional descriptions of a god's-
eye view of a squalid human world:

The office of the New York Eclipse *was at the top of an immense
building on Broadway. It was a sheer mountain to the heights of which
the interminable thunder of the streets arose faintly. . . . At the foot of
the cliff lay City Hall Park. It seemed no larger than a quilt. The grey
walks patterned the snow-covering into triangles and ovals and upon
them many tiny people scurried here and there without sound, like fish
at the bottom of a pool. It was only the vehicles that sent high,
unmistakably, the deep bass of their movement. And yet after listening
one seemed to hear a singular murmurous note, a pulsation, as if the
crowd made noise by its mere living, a mellow hum of the eternal strife.*
[3:123–24]

So high, in fact, that sometimes only sounds drift up from the noisy human world to grace the godlike ears.

Mostly, however, *Active Service* is, as Crane wrote and Levenson has noted, a parodic novel "full of love and war." What has not been stressed is that the novel occasionally draws specific parallels to Love and War, that is, to Aphrodite and Ares, the most notorious lovers in classical mythology, and among the most psychologically interesting. Crane fails to develop the psychology, but he is specifically aware of both the astronomical and the classical implications of this love and war novel, for Coleman says on his way to Greece: "Love and war—war and Marjory—were in conjunction—both in Greece—and he could tilt with one lance at both gods" (3:157).

Traditionally seen as a quarrelsome, hard-drinking, fast-gambling, gore-loving mass of passions, Ares also manages at times to be a cool and efficient general. Crane lends these attributes to Coleman both before and after the latter specifically and grammatically associates himself with the less pleasant half of the "war and love, war and Marjory" combination. Coleman is thinking about the Greco-Turkish War, but since the reader sees so little of that war, and since Coleman brings his warlike passions with him to Greece, Coleman is War in this novel: Greece is merely his familiar background. If Coleman is not quite the "gambling drunkard" that Professor Wainwright thinks he is, it is nevertheless true that Coleman is a "drinking gambler." Seemingly rejected by Marjory, Coleman immediately distinguishes himself from "old fashioned lovers" who "languish" when rejected by calling himself a "modern lover" who gets "drunk": "When yesterday, the dagger of disappointment was driven deep into my heart, I immediately played poker hard as I could and incidentally got loaded" (3:141). Although he spends most of the novel drinking or about to drink or having just drunk, he is also described throughout in military terms as one whose "face was lit with something of the self-contained enthusiasm of a general" (3:130), and who "in a few brisk sentences" could "set a complex machine in motion": "His men no longer thrilled with admiration at the precision with which he grasped each obligation of the campaign toward a successful edition" (3:129). Finally, like Ares, a yellow journalist must have an eye for blood and gore in a news story "as a morsel to be flung at a ravenous public" (3:128).

More than ten pages later Coleman is still playing cards and drinking when he gets the idea to go to Greece. Only Zeus could be expected to understand that when Ares wants to rest he looks for a war somewhere. Coleman's boss does not understand this from Coleman: "I know there is likely to be a war there. But I think that is exactly what would rest me" (3:144). Only Ares and Coleman "would go to bed and think of war" (3:157).

While Ares and Coleman can be relatively consistent, Aphrodite is a more complex figure. She is sometimes portrayed as a demure virgin representing idealized and chaste love, and sometimes as a sensuous pleasure-seeker representing sensuous pleasure-seeking. Marjory Wainwright is a pale version of the first ("Simpy," Levenson calls her), and Nora Black, a modern version of the second. Aside from Ares, the most important man in Aphrodite's life is Hephaestus, the ugly blacksmith of the gods, whom Aphrodite reluctantly married. While Coke is not physically crippled as was Hephaestus, he is like the god in his ill-tempered, bad-mannered, loutish behavior. It is also interesting to note that coke makes a very hot fire for a forge.

Little need be said about Marjory Wainwright as the virginal Aphrodite. Coleman associates her with the planet Venus (war and love were "in conjunction") and with the goddess for which the planet was named. Only one other time is she directly related to a goddess and that occurs when the narrator describes Coleman's elation when a stopped train begins moving again: "He was elated as if in his abjection his beloved's hand had reached to him from the clouds" (3:139). Otherwise, Marjory might as well be a statue of Aphrodite for all she adds to the novel and for all the interest we have in her. Once, in fact, when he is leading the party toward safety and they stop and rest, Coleman puts a blanket around Marjory: "It was something like putting a wrap about the shoulders of a statue" (3:197); elsewhere, her face "looked simply of lovely marble" (3:201). At another time, "she had exhibited about as much recognition of him as would a stone fountain" (3:198). At places like these, *Active Service* becomes a parody of itself; because she is a statue, Coleman "loved her more." Aphrodite, perhaps, but remote and nearly as cold as an idea.

Anything but an idea, Nora Black figures too briefly in the book. Easily the most interesting character, she seems to have at least two roles: one, as the Aphroditic foil to Marjory and her rival for Coleman; and two, after Coleman first rejects her, as a kind of Artemis-like warrior who attempts to win Coleman in a stereotypically "feminine" love battle. As a goddess of love, Nora would seem to have it all; she is beautiful, sensuous, witty, and very lively. When she tries to seduce Coleman in a room of her apartment that "used to be part of a harem long ago" (3:226), she wears a dress of "Grecian silk" that is "the color of new straw." Add soft lights, four magnums of chilled champagne, an orris root and violet perfume. Nora knows her business so well that no one could seriously consider her to be a virgin unless she is to be associated with Aphrodite, who, owing to her special powers, is able to renew her virginity by bathing and is thus able to be both lover and virgin. So, too, it would seem, for Nora, who is twice referred to as Aphrodite, as that "splendid and fabulous virgin" (3:227, 229).

In her Grecian silk, the "splendid and fabulous virgin" is at the point of conquering Ares, who is watching her with eyes of "steel colored flames" (Nora prefers a man "with steel in him" [3:156]), when she makes an irrevocable error in reminding Coleman of Marjory: "Don't you think I'm just as nice as Marjory?" (3:229). Coleman leaves Nora, who must now change her tactics. The next time she appears, it is clear that she has completely altered her approach, for now she is less like Aphrodite and more like Artemis or Hippolyta, a female warrior and counterpart to Ares. For the remainder of the novel she spends her time trying to drive a wedge between Coleman and Marjory: "In her manner was all the confidence of an old warrior, a veteran, who addresses the universe with assurance because of his past battles" (3:243–44).

In the end the classics professor's daughter triumphs by doing nothing; by doing nothing, the novel fails. Coleman opts for respectability, conservatism, tradition—the statue of Aphrodite, but not the real thing. If Stallman is right in suggesting that Nora is based on Cora, and he probably is, then Crane at least chose the real thing.

If Crane chose the woman that Coleman did not, is the novel a commonplace version of "The Jolly Corner"? Did Crane write an idealized and sentimental version of what he might have done but did not? If so, then perhaps Levenson is right. Perhaps in writing about the public vision of himself, Crane succumbed to the public vision of himself. Perhaps the writing of *Active Service* is partly the "depressing story of a young man with inadequate resources, intellectual and cultural even more than economic, giving way before the institutional pressures of his time."

No one can deny the debilitating power of economic pressures, but one may question the notion that Crane lacked the intellect and the cultural heritage with which to stand up to "institutional pressures." Certainly, the novel becomes a parody of itself, but that in itself is not necessarily aesthetically bad; *The Red Badge* parodies itself and few complain. It is entirely possible that Crane was simply unable to carry off a grand spoof of the love and adventure novel in which he could have his money and his integrity as well. Much of the disparagement of the novel and of Crane's motives rests with his use of "active service" as a title. Levenson says that this "military term asserts a maximum claim for journalists in the war zone" (3:xliii) and implies that Crane's motives were commercial, not private. Probably so, but it is also possible that Crane gives himself an intellectual and aesthetic, albeit morally equivocal, way out of the charge of commercialism when he describes Coleman as War battling with Love: "He was on active service, an active service of the heart" (3:187).

The cultural resources were there: Crane had an entire classical mythology to work with in plotting his novel of love and war. But just as certainly, he did not use those resources. The novel is banal and trite, but one need not blame intellect and culture. Crane never wrote well about the middle class in general or what Fiedler calls "dark ladies" and "snow maidens" in particular. It is bad for the old reasons: health and finances. Crane began the novel late in 1897, when he was still fairly healthy and when his finances did not yet seem impossibly out of control. Perhaps during this time he wrote the first and best chapters of the book. The effects of the fever he got in Cuba and the consumption that was flaring up began taking their toll long before he finished the novel in May of 1899, and his finances were in terrible shape at this time. Increased debt and increased illness had much more to do with making *Active Service* a bad novel than did intellectual and cultural resources, both of which Crane had in abundance. We can only plead with Crane: "May heaven forgive it for being so bad."[29]

The Old World has had the poems of myths,
fictions, feudalism, conquest, caste, dynastic
wars, and splendid exceptional characters
and affairs, which have been great; but the
New World needs the poems of realities.

WHITMAN

"A Backward Glance o'er Travel'd Roads"

And not to have is the beginning of desire.
You must become an ignorant man again
And see the sun again with an ignorant eye
And see it clearly in the idea of it.

STEVENS

"Notes toward a Supreme Fiction"

Chapter Four

This Booming Chaos: Crane's Search for Transcendence

Traveling Inward

Stephen Crane was nearly a writer of epic. Certainly he wrote the great American epic into *The Red Badge*, but then he wrote it out again, mocking accepted notions of heroism central to Western consciousness. Crane depicted archetypes of unconsciousness very early in his career, particularly in the Sullivan County, New York City, and Asbury Park sketches, where he approached transcendence only occasionally, as in "Killing His Bear." Transcendence, when it appears, tends to exist in the stories separate from and unperceived by the protagonists, as in "The Reluctant Voyagers." Later, in *Maggie*, Crane scoffed at the idea that any world existed except the material, and his scoffing was aided by his use of a classical hierarchy of gods and goddesses of heaven (Sol and Phaethon) and hell (Dis and Proserpina) to mock ideas about transcendence to either higher or lower planes of existence—one of the reasons, as Gullason explains, that *Maggie* fails as a tragedy.[1] After writing *The Red Badge* Crane traveled west for Bacheller's Syndicate in 1895 and saw for himself what Frederick Jackson Turner was showing: the frontier was closed. Possessed like any other American by the myth of manifest destiny, Crane nevertheless knew that the myth had been invalidated. Consequently, his western stories portray the demise of an almost heroic, nearly Homeric society. Into the garden of Crane's idea of the West had come the machine: a society of Pullmans, electric streetcars, businessmen, and progress. If the former was naive, bombastic, and childishly honest, the latter was insidious, conspiratorial, and corrupt.

The West encompassed an irony interesting to Crane: the early western society was old to the world but new to white America; the society that replaced it was relatively new to the world but old to the United States. By blending these histories with classical allusions and genres Crane revitalized and universalized his theme and its ironies. The American West was simply the latest example of the recurring death of an ageless dream of possibility, of starting anew in a new land, a dream possessed by most epic heroes. To take the epic to task on its own terms is a requirement for writers of epic, but then to attempt systematically to destroy the epic's claim to veracity is perhaps unprecedented. To the degree that he succeeded, Crane may have called in question beliefs about myth, history, religion, government, and perhaps many of mankind's other cultural foundations.

During 1897 and 1898, when most of his great short stories were written, Crane's interest in exposing cultural aspects of epic to ridicule begins to diminish and in some works his obvious use of traditional epic lessens. Certainly, those devices of epic which stood him in good stead in *The Red Badge* do not disappear entirely; still, one of the less cultural elements of epic always more or less present in his work begins to accrue comparatively more importance: the requirement that the protagonist face death squarely and by doing so overcome it. Transcendence seems to result more from the protagonist's individual strengths than from his cultural strengths. "The Open Boat," written shortly after Crane was shipwrecked in January of 1897, and "Death and the Child," published not long after Crane first saw battle in the Greco-Turkish War of 1897, illustrate this shift in Crane's interests from cultural to individual (or psychological) aspects of epic. Manifest destiny takes a turn in Crane and begins to look for a way to conquer the "other" by mastering the self.

To be sure, "The Open Boat" repudiates traditional epic, and the repudiation begins, as is common for Crane's stories, with the first paragraph:

None of them knew the color of the sky. Their eyes glanced level, and were fastened upon the waves that swept toward them. These waves were of the hue of slate, save for the tops, which were of foaming white, and all of the men knew the color of the sea. The horizon narrowed and widened, and dipped and rose, and at all times the edge was jagged with waves that seemed to thrust up in points like rocks. [5:68]

The main thrust of the paragraph is that these four men are utterly absorbed by the sea, or, in terms of the epic of consciousness, that they are battling an archetype of unconsciousness. The first sentence is pointedly after-the-fact and contributes both to the notion of the men's absorption and to the idea they they are bereft, permanently or temporarily, of those qualities symbolized by the sky: light, knowledge, consciousness. While the first is Crane's most often quoted sentence, its complement is seldom mentioned, even though it is at least as important as the first: "all of the men knew the color of the sea." There may be, as well, in the simile of the waves as rocks a deliberate allusion to the famous Wandering, or Clashing, Rocks of Homer's *Odyssey* and Apollonius's *Argonautica*.

On one level a perfectly accurate and impressionistic description, on another level the paragraph's last sentence serves as a literary allusion supporting shifting reference points on and above the water. Occasionally in Greek epics heroes lose their frame of reference. Odysseus, for example, temporarily loses sight of his goal while a captive in Calypso's cave. More specifically, he and, earlier, the Argonauts of Apollonius's epyllion temporarily lose sight of the sky while they pass through the tented waves of the Wandering Rocks. Crane could have chosen this allusion for many reasons, but one of the most important may have been that it depicts a moment during a sea journey when, even in classical epics, what appears to be true is not. The difference between these Greek works and Crane's is that in the former the condition is temporary, while the language of "The Open Boat" suggests that man may be permanently benighted. The *Odyssey*, the *Argonautica*, and "The Open Boat" concern a quest for "home," but only in "The Open Boat" does the quest seem to be futile. Odysseus knows he will reach home. Most of the Argonauts, informed by various oracles or by such signs from the sky as birds, stars, and thunderings, know they will return. Some know they will not. Even ancient audiences knew who would and who would not survive. The men in the dingey have no such assurance. And the reader is assured only of the survival of one to tell the story.

"The Open Boat" is extremely inclusive, for it seems that not only classical epics, but Christian ones as well, specifically Dante's *Inferno*, are targets for Crane's irony, as Kenneth Reed has shown. The point of allusions and parallels to classical and Christian epic in "The Open Boat" may be to invert the epics' original intensions. This would be consistent with Crane's earlier uses of epic allusions. "The Open Boat" may provide, as Reed says, "a dramatic illustration of the naturalist's rejection of the fundamental principle that human experience may lead to moral certainty."[2]

This view, described by Gerstenberger as "epistemological existentialism," makes "The Open Boat" a story about "man's inability to know anything about the complex whole of existence."[3] The story may be explained epically in exactly the same terms as *The Red Badge*. Having sloughed off cultural beliefs in the first two-thirds of the story—there are "no bricks and no temples"—the correspondent comes finally to a confrontation with death, and the narrator relates it in the present tense as a purely existential reflection: "Perhaps an individual must consider his own death to be the final phenomenon of nature" (5:91). At this point in the story the correspondent faces death and perhaps achieves a kind of transcendence. Unceremoniously dumped into the sea, that grand archetype of the unconscious, and yet utterly conscious at the same time, the correspondent is momentarily caught in an undertow and considers his own death. His achieving this conscious unconsciousness, during which his mind revolves like a man in a maelstrom around the question of his own death, would seem to be much like Henry Fleming's discovery of heroism in *The Red Badge*: man has transcended nature by transcending himself. Moreover, if the ending of the story is as ironical as it is lyrical—and some have pointed out that lyricism in Crane signals irony—then the correspondent, like Henry, also forgets what he has learned; the idea that they can then "be interpreters" is absurd: "When it came night, the white waves paced to and fro in the moonlight, and the wind brought the sound of the great sea's voice to the men on shore, and they felt that they could then be interpreters" (5:92).

But "The Open Boat" is, as Conrad said, "a symbolic tale." It is also so finely shaped that it tends to act as a prism for almost any well-polished and intelligent interpretation to penetrate and yield a finely ordered array of colors. This quality alone would make the story, for Aristotle, Crane's best; it is so inclusive as to support an opposite interpretation from that discussed here. One which concludes that the men do learn and which further illuminates Crane's use of epic is that summarized by J. C. Levenson, who discusses the story in terms of "the fiction of consciousness": "'The Open Boat' is . . . a movement toward understanding. Technically, the fiction of consciousness simply makes dramatically immediate the way things felt. . . . Formally . . . there are cumulative changes whereby men, though they cannot control what happens, can at least come to a rational perception of their fate" (5:lxvi–lxvii).

The last paragraph can be looked at differently under this light. The paragraph is lyrical because true: the interpretation of the men lies in the content of nature: white waves, moonlight, the "great sea's voice," *and* the imaginative construct of the paragraph, which creates beauty and order and value in a meaningless universe. Here, then, the transcendence is permanent, or at least has the capability of being permanent.[4] As Levenson puts it:

The expansion of consciousness leads at last to the encounter with that absolute finality, the extinction of consciousness. The progress from self-engrossment to clear vision, from fanciful outrage to puzzled acceptance, is a growth of moral intelligence which does not simply come from within. The encounter with reality has made a crucial difference. From it the men learn. . . . *Self-mastery and self-knowledge come only with the capacity to interpret the world outside oneself. [5:lxviii]*

Levenson has described not only "The Open Boat" here, but also a prerequisite for epic transcendence. The only addition to be made is that Levenson's last sentence is reversible for epic: the capacity to interpret the world outside oneself comes only with self-mastery and self-knowledge. Drained of all physical strength, immersed in the unconscious energy of the sea, the correspondent reflects unconsciousness through his repetitions, his chants of "Can it be possible? Can it be possible?" An extraordinary consciousness is conveyed by his reflecting upon his death as nature's "final phenomenon."

Crane throws bricks at cultural temples in "The Open Boat," but soon discovering that "there are no bricks and no temples," he spends more time than ever before facing the prerequisite for transcendence: death. He also advances from the clear denunciation of a lasting epic transcendence in *The Red Badge* to the deliberate ambivalence of "The Open Boat." The question is: Is the last paragraph ironic?

Separated from the rest of the canon, "The Open Boat" remains beautifully ambivalent. And since everything to come before that story clearly repudiates lasting epic transcendence, it would be nice to accept Levenson's reading that the "men do learn," and learn permanently. There are two problems with this interpretation, sound as it may be. First, as Griffith shows, all of Crane's lyrical endings earlier than "The Open Boat" are patently ironic:[5] *Maggie, The Red Badge,* and "The Veteran" to cite only three. Second, "Death and the Child," a story which follows "The Open Boat" chronologically as one of his greatest and which also follows the pattern of the epic of consciousness, provides an ending more devastatingly ironic in terms of epic and nihilistic in terms of life than any of Crane's other works: Peza is Crane's Kurtz, albeit a pale copy, for Peza has only imagined the horror. If transcendence occurred in "Death and the Child," there would be grounds for accepting a "transcendent" interpretation of "The Open Boat" as *the* interpretation. But since there are none, it is difficult to exclude the possibility that the ending of "The Open Boat" is ironic.

If Crane is finally able to deal at length with the existential heart of epic—facing death—in "The Open Boat" in part because he had come so close to death, he is able perhaps to pursue the subject again in "Death and the Child" because of what he saw in Greece only four months after his experience off Datona Beach. Greece was another disillusionment for Crane, much like his trip west, but even more so. Holton suggests that Crane first retreated from staring at reality as a result of his Greek experiences, having discovered there that "war is only an instinctive killing, conducted and then marveled at by a gawking crowd. For the sensitive man . . . like Crane . . . there is only one possible response. From this intolerable reality he can only turn away."[6]

It is possible that Crane also turned away even further from his classical sources because of this experience. "I'd a great idea of Greece," he said after returning to England from reporting what was then popularly known as the Thirty Days' War but is now called the Greco-Turkish War of 1897: "Say, when I planted those hoofs of mine on Greek soil, I felt like the hull of Greek literature."[7] If the past tense is significant in contrasting his feelings before with those after his first war experience, then it would be safe to say that the "great idea of Greece" had been shattered. Certainly the Greek nation was, because from about mid-April through mid-May of 1897 Greek forces were routed on all fronts, largely, if not exclusively, through the apparent incompetence and inexperience of the Greek rulers. Retreat after seemingly needless retreat was ordered, often from nearly impregnable positions and occasionally long before Turkish forces arrived at the scene. Only one of many examples, "Crane at Velestino" (9:19–23) provides a barely controlled description of Crane's own private disappointment at Greece's national disgrace:

I hoped the Greeks on the plain would hurry and drive the Turks from their position. They did this gallantly in a short, ferocious infantry fight in the woods. The bit of woods seemed to be on fire. After a great rattling and banging the Turks went out. After this attack and defeat there was general rejoicing along the Greek lines and satisfaction all over. The officers walked proudly, the men in the trenches grinned. Then, mind you, just at this time, late in the afternoon, after another successful day, came orders to retreat. . . . I send this from Volo and before you print it the Turks will be here.

On another occasion, in "The Blue Badge of Cowardice" (9:44–48), Crane expressed it succinctly, angrily, and outright, almost as if he himself had been personally insulted: "Back fell the Greek army, wrathful, sullen, fierce as any victorious army would be when commanded to retreat before the enemy it had defeated." Crane is clearly on the side of Greece; of that nation and its literature he clearly had "a great idea."

Crane's disillusionment takes other and varied forms throughout his war reports from Greece, and many times, its form is one of contrast between the Greece of which he had had "a great idea" and the Greece he saw before him. In describing "a certain part of the Greek nature" foreign to "the Anglo-Saxon," Crane mentions "a battery of howitzers on a hill above the mosque and the bullet-swept square. The captain of this battery walked out to his position at middle-rear. He addressed his men. His chest was well out, and his manner was gorgeous. If one could have judged by the tone, it was one of the finest speeches of the age. It was Demosthenes returned and in command of a battery of howitzers" (9:32–33). William Spofford locates "more than fifty-five instances" of Crane's using or describing oratory.[8] In every instance, insincerity is implied, along with puffery, egotism, and lying. Dredging up Demosthenes for this comparison would indicate that already Crane's idea of ancient Greece was being modified by what he was seeing of its modern counterpart, but it also sheds a certain classical light on Crane's considerable use of the notion of oratory in other works, particularly *The Red Badge*.

Still, on the rare occasion that Crane could report even a minor victory, as toward the end of "A Fragment of Velestino" (9:27–44), his positive image of Greece is reinforced by the centuries that lay behind Greek civilization and pervaded, for example, the evening after a victorious day. Reading the description immediately evokes Greek shepherds resting above the plains of Troy:

There were some mountaineer volunteers in great woolly grey shepherds' cloaks. They were curious figures in the evening light, perfectly romantic if it were not for the modernity of the rifles and the shining lines of cartridges. With the plain a sea of shadow below them, these men sang softly the wild minor ballads of the hills. As the evening deepened many men . . . slept, but these grey-cloaked mountaineers continued to sing. . . . They sang of war, and their songs were new to the sense, reflecting the centuries of their singing, and as the ultimate quiet of night came to the height this low chanting was the only sound. [9:44]

In "Death and the Child," a youth named Peza becomes caught up in this Greek war song, only to have its tempo change to that of a horrifying dirge. Initially meeting a young veteran officer who, as Eric Solomon says, "accepts the role of Virgil to Peza's Dante,"[9] Peza is guided to "the top of a great hill," where he begins observing the inferno below: "Before them was a green plain as level as an inland sea" (5:124). Like the ocean of "The Open Boat," this "inland sea," this battlefield, provides the archetype of unconsciousness, the "cave" of "Death and the Child." Surrounded by mountains, the plain also contains "little black lines from which floated slanting sheets of smoke. . . . It was war" (5:124–135). Although Peza here does much observing, and no doubt becomes more conscious as a result (he is "edified, aghast, triumphant"), Peza is less prescient than the narrator who mocks him: "It was not a battle to the nerves. One could survey it [the battlefield] with equanimity, as if it were a tea-table" (5:124–25).

So Peza "bounded" down the hill toward the battle. The young officer finally leaves Peza with some soldiers at a place where there may soon be some heavy fighting. In the process Peza learns several things: (1) "the accidental destruction of an individual, Peza by name, would perhaps be nothing at all"; (2) that his death "would be as romantic, to the old standards, as death by a bit of falling iron in a factory"; (3) that the peasant soldiers were generally much more calm than he; (4) that after entering the battle zone, acting like "a corpse walking on the bottom of the sea," and conceding that the wounded men may, like him, have "dreamed at lightning speed until the capacity for it was overwhelmed" (5:130), he finally realizes that "pity had a numerical limit." He no longer says, "those poor people," as he had in the beginning. Peza has a vision of finally reaching the "bottom of the abyss" when he finds himself below the battle: "In the vale there was an effect as if one was then beneath the battle. It was going on above somewhere. Alone, unguided, Peza felt like a man groping in a cellar."

That there is no transcendence, temporary or otherwise, in "Death and the Child" is made clear by the fact that Peza runs, like Henry, only never to return. Moreover, Henry had run from a real danger, an enemy with guns. Peza runs from an hallucination about dead men. Still, Peza's vision is much more horrifying than Henry Fleming's. And last, there occurs one of Crane's final descriptions of hell, a description more horrifying in the circumstances than those hells described in "An Experiment in Misery," *Maggie*, *The Red Badge*, and several other stories. It is also more obviously classical. Having come to a place where he might soon be in battle, Peza is armed with a dead man's rifle, which has the "crawling and frightful"movements of a "serpent" (5:139), and the cartridge bandoleer of another, which makes him feel "that the dead man had flung his two arms around him" (5:138). All dressed up for war with rifle, shells, and a new white hat, Peza faces the final confrontation which must be overcome before transcendence is possible:

He looked behind him, and saw that a head by some chance had been uncovered from its blanket. Two liquid-like eyes were staring into his face. The head was turned a little sideways as if to get a better opportunity for the scrutiny. Peza could feel himself blanch; he was being drawn and drawn by these dead men slowly, firmly down as to some mystical chamber under the earth where they could walk, fearful

*figures, swollen and blood-marked. He was bidden; they had com-
manded him; he was going, going, going.*
  . . . the man in the new white hat bolted for the rear. [5:139]

If Peza had lost some "egotism" by obeying the young officer's commands, he would have been annihilated by obeying these commandments, but perhaps would have achieved a kind of transcendence. But he doesn't, and once again Crane exhibits his fundamental belief that "conceit is the very engine of life."

Peza survives, climbing the mountain again, but neither pretending to see that the world was a world "for him," as does Henry Fleming, nor thinking that he could then be an "interpreter," but rather to lie gasping "in the manner of a fish" (5:141).

The child who had watched the battle from afar and who had been throughout a human personification of nature—indifferent or at most mildly interested in the goings on in the valley—is also a more devastating symbol in that he is probably doomed to repeat Peza's experience, as are all children in any age. When the child asks "Are you a man?" the answer is clearly "yes." Crane's idea of the human condition has changed. Henry Fleming, for example, is defeated because he can't sustain his vision. According to Holton, on the other hand, "it is Peza's very capacity to apprehend which has defeated and dehumanized him."[10] One can agree that Peza is defeated by his apprehensions without believing that he has also been dehumanized by them. The human condition seems to be one of confronting reality and then running from it in horror. The act of facing the horror and transcending makes epic heroes heroes, because in doing so they become somewhat more than human. It is in the failure, in the tragedy of not quite transcending reality after the pain and struggle, that one is reminded of the hero's humanity.

When Crane returned from reporting the Greco-Turkish

War, he said that *The Red Badge* "is all right."[11] But it wasn't, for the very metaphor that manifests Henry Fleming's heroism— his impression of an individual blade of grass—becomes the metaphor for Peza's defeat: Peza "knew that the definition of his misery could be written on a wee grass-blade" (5:141).

Turning Outward

After "The Open Boat" and "Death and the Child," Crane either grew tired of his self-imposed task of exposing the innumerable illusions by which men live or he began to see possibilities in a new area based more upon affirmation than upon denial. After his Greek experience, he seemed never again to be so sure of himself. Perhaps he could not be sure that even his repudiations had been correct. To deny the epic, for example, requires certainty that the epic is wrong. In life, one may proceed by saying that something is or is not true, but Crane's art of denial, his repudiations of the accumulated assumptions of millennia, becomes ambivalent in "The Open Boat" and downright horrifying in "Death and the Child." Perhaps Holton is right and Crane "turned away," but perhaps Crane simply no longer had a strong commitment to the belief that certain things were false.

Whatever the reason, Crane's quarrel with epic and its illusions disappears from his work after 1898, and he seems to have spent his remaining time, as Stallman and Liebling say, either writing the sort of thing that would get him out of debt or casting about in a somewhat confused attempt to work his way out of artistic uncertainty.[12] Much may be accounted for by the simple fact that after reporting the Spanish-American War, Crane was very sick. Even more than in the earlier stories, a riot of shifting points of view, wrong interpretations, and unanswered questions fill the later stories. "War Memories," for example, lacks any epic background, and yet its sentences are continually placed in the interrogative, more so even than in *The Red Badge*.

The difference is that the unifying power of epic is gone.

By repudiating the epic and all it stands for—nationalism, patriotism, the greatness of individual and collective man, the existence of supernatural powers that care and protect and guide—Crane, in his life and in his best work, faced the horror of a meaningless universe as squarely as anyone has. That he took no respite, in spite of malaria and tuberculosis, is perhaps unparalleled. It probably shortened his life.

While few deny that Crane's art broke down after the great period of 1897 to early 1898, some of the later pieces may illuminate where he might have gone had he lived long enough to pick up the pieces. Since Crane apparently belonged to the group of American writers whose "quest for a supreme fiction" is a driving force, he had to go beyond his repudiations. Although the lines are far from clear-cut, the evident distinction between his best works and the lesser, particularly the later, works indicates that he did. The best works tend to conform to a definition of modernism given by Altieri: modern literature tends, albeit often negatively, toward "impersonality (i.e., formalism, overtly mythical [epical] themes and constructs, the use of persona, and a stress on complex and paradoxical statements)."[13] Nagel has said that "the interpretive uncertainties of [Crane's] Impressionism foreshadow . . . much of Post-Modernism."[14] While perceptive and true, this observation is so in part because both impressionism and modernism foreshadow the postmodern revolt. Crane is impressionistic throughout his career, and in that sense is postmodern. But Crane's great works, to the degree that they fit period definitions, are modern. His often bad later works tend to fit Altieri's definition of postmodernism as a movement emphasizing "the direct, the personal, the local, the anti-formal, and the topical."

Formalism in Crane—his use of myth, epic, and literary tradition in general—has been the subject of this book, but his use of persona and paradox are also well known. Maggie is not Crane, nor, certainly, is Henry Fleming, and while the correspondent in the dingey is in a way a Crane stand-in, he is so only as one undergoing the experience. The narrator of "The Open Boat," on the other hand, is the after-the-fact presence. The correspondent is decidedly a persona.

The personae of the best works tend to give way later to Crane surrogates, especially in some of the war stories, where the line between journalism and fiction grows fuzzy: Little Nell, Shackles, Johnnie, and Vernall.[15] In "Marines Signaling under Fire at Guantanamo" (6:194–200), even the surrogate is removed and the narrator is "I." While the "direct" tone advanced by some of these characters may be a result of the stories' closeness to newspaper dispatches, that tone does not necessarily explain such direct addresses to the reader as appear, for example, at the end of "War Memories": "The episode is closed. And you can depend upon it that I have told you nothing at all, nothing at all, nothing at all" (6:263).

"War Memories" also exposes some of Crane's rare personal moods, moods which sometimes verge on a nineteenth-century equivalent to contemporary "confessional" poetry. Most of Crane's readers knew who he was, knew he was covering the war, and could be expected to assume that Vernall, the "I" of the story and a correspondent, was Crane. What Vernall says is accurate, but not the kind of thing one reported about oneself to a nation sending the cream of its youth off to lick the Spanish. Having just made friends with one of those fine young men, a surgeon named Gibbs, Vernall soon finds Gibbs shot and dying, "dying hard. It took him a long time to die. . . . I thought this man would never die. I wanted him to die" (6:226–27). This statement is very personal, almost embarrassing in print even today, but certainly accurate. Yet it has little in it of the desire to shock so common in Crane, although that can be found easily enough even in the late writing.[16] Later he describes his great fear at the prospect of going on patrol the next day: "All that night I was afraid. Bitterly afraid. In the morning I wished for some mild attack of disease, something that would incapacitate me for the business of going out gratuitously to be bombarded" (6:228). Much of the remainder of the story is a description of fear and ineffectiveness. Crane was beginning, in the war stories drawn from experience, to write in a new subjective voice, so much so that he was often parodied for, of all things, egotism:

> *I have seen a battle.*
> *I find it is very like what*
> *I wrote up before.*
> *I congratulate myself that*
> *I ever saw a battle.*
> *I am pleased with the sound of war.*[17]

On occasion, however, Crane can be both personal and classical. That is, he can describe war in his own voice and be directly allusive, as in this description from "War Memories," where the correspondent has "a fine view of the Spanish lines": "There was a man in a Panama hat strolling to and fro behind one of the Spanish trenches, gesticulating at times with a walking stick! That was the strangest sight of my life—that symbol, that quaint figure of Mars. . . . He mystified us all" (6:245).

Perhaps what prompted many of the parodies was not Crane's egotism, although it was interpreted in this way, but rather the "anarchic individualism" so fundamental to postmodernism and vitally basic to Crane. His rejection of Christianity in *Maggie*, of literature and history in *The Red Badge*, of culture in *The Monster*, and of everything else in "The Open Boat" and "Death and the Child," and his insistence upon retaining what he called "the anarchy" of *The Black Riders*, attest convincingly to the ultimate rightness of Crane's confession to Nellie Crouse that he was "by inclination a wild, shaggy barbarian." A barbarian, too, in the classical Greek sense of "foreigner," Crane seemed always more at home walking the line between the anarchy of nihilism and the totalitarianism of late nineteenth-century American society; he seems to have been a cousin of chaos who only visited with mankind, a species to which at times he seems only distantly related.

The clearest tie between Crane and the postmodern, however, lies in the manner in which he falls directly in line with the tradition of American literature beginning, at least, with Whitman and moving to Wallace Stevens and beyond. In *The Fragile Presence*, Killinger speaks to the issue of the quest for a supreme fiction when he says that "the quest for a new transcendence *in* and *through* the materialities of human existence is unspeakably important."[18] In America this quest is perhaps first clearly articulated by Whitman—"The New World needs poems of realities"—most vividly stated by Stevens in "Not Ideas about the Thing but the Thing Itself"— and, according to Altieri, now resides in the "postmodern insistence that value is not mediated but stems from a direct engagement with the universal forces of being manifest in the particular."[19] In short, Crane's impressionism throughout most of his career deliberately and painfully avoids the notion of value; toward the end, that impressionism can be said to create it just as deliberately: a clear and direct movement in Crane from what became an aspect of modernism to what has been called an "insistence" of postmodernism.

A prerequisite for unmediated experience lies in a process Roy Harvey Pearce and others have called "decreation."

Crane's art of repudiating epic is a holistic attempt to decreate not only literature but all human values: "human forms must first be destroyed if we are to be open to the true sources of value manifest in the natural process which create forms."[20] This, perhaps, is the ultimate goal of Crane's impressionism.

Attempts to participate in unmediated reality by finding some certainty in impressionistic experiences are everywhere in Crane; the complement of such participation, the extinction of ego, a special concern of much postmodernism, with rare exceptions comes late in Crane's career, for he first had to dispense with the egotistical selflessness of patriotism and the prideful humility of religion, as well as the egotism and pride necessary to one who undertook these repudiations. Mediated experiences with reality are everywhere in Crane and almost always provide sources for illusion and distortion. The old chieftain, long a British captive, in "The King's Favor" engages in this sort of illusion when he hears an old war song and has a vision of killing the British and being "again a great chief" (8:571). This story tries to evoke from readers, says Bergon, "those very states of wonder, awe, or transcendence which [Crane] habitually attributes to his characters."[21] Similarly, Maggie's "dream garden," Henry's Christian-inspired "visions of cruelty," and his Homeric pictures of deeds "paraded in wide purple and gold" are part of experience mediated by imagination and memory.

Occasionally, Crane presented impressionistic pictures that seem to have come close to passing beyond mediation. The early "Killing His Bear" describes a killing this way: "The little man saw the swirling fur over his gun barrel. The earth faded to nothing. Only space and game, the aim and the hunted. Mad emotions powerful enough to rock worlds, hurled through the little man, but did not shake the tiniest nerve" (8:251). Henry's vision of grass blades is another: "His mind took a mechanical but firm impression." There is mystery in all this. Scratchy is awed by his "glimpse at another world," and perhaps the Swede's "supreme cry of astonishment" is likewise partly the result of such a vision. Except for the earliest, in which the little man afterwards "ran up and kicked the ribs of the bear," these visions invariably produce selflessness. The Swede, in Frye's terminology, becomes a lightning rod for humanity. Scratchy relents: "I 'low it's off, Jack." And Henry, immediately after experiencing his one clear vision, leads the charge with a "delirium that encounters despair and death, and is heedless and blind to the odds. It is a temporary but sublime absence of selfishness" (2:105).

Selflessness, a manifestation of what psycho-criticism rather unnecessarily calls "ego annihilation" and "id destruction," mystified Crane. It seems to have been the one human quality he could not explain through his theory that "conceit" was "the very engine of life": "The final wall," he said on his deathbed, "is human kindness."[22] In postmodern literature selflessness is largely antihumanistic or nonhumanistic, but in Crane the question of whether it is humanistic or not is difficult to answer. To the degree that Crane is romantic, selflessness becomes antihumanistic. When he is being classical, it is, of course, humanistic. At such moments one must return to the picture of the "conceited" Swede outside the Palace Hotel. It is a picture, a metaphor for all of Crane's work: man implacably struggling against chaos, against the other.

There is no transcendence in Crane's work. In epic terms, the struggle is solely for consciousness; finally for Crane, transcending consciousness is not transcendence but a falling back and succumbing to false echoes in caves of unconsciousness. Still, in spite of this nihilistic view, there are numerous instances in the later stories of a kind of acceptance of man's struggle against "this booming chaos" (6:196). War is business. War is Henry Fleming "at a task . . . like a carpenter who has made many boxes, making still another box, only there was great haste in his movements" (2:35). If Henry and the narrator seem repelled by this "business," the later war stories project the business of war with a sense of awesome mystery; it can even become very personal and "sublime":

There wasn't a high heroic face among them. They were all men intent on business. That was all. It may seem that I am trying to make everything a squalor. That would be wrong. I feel that things were often sublime. But they were differently sublime. They were not of our shallow and preposterous fictions. They stood out in a simple, majestic commonplace. It was the behavior of men. In one way, each man was just pegging along. . . . In another way it was pageantry, the pageantry of the accomplishment of naked duty. [6:249]

Although Crane manages to skewer "preposterous fictions," he is not primarily concerned with them, but rather with those men honestly, completely, "earnestly at work" (6:232).

The self-sacrifice and inexplicable kindnesses performed by men for no other reason than that they do perform them caused Crane to face a spectacle in which resentment toward a material and indifferent universe simply falls away, as does the antihumanism of romantic and postmodern visions. Crane at last comes as close to an epic transcendence as he ever does, and he does it by throwing away his art, much as Dante does when the character Dante arrives at the gates of paradise and is unable to describe it in words. Here is Crane: "One cannot speak of it—the spectacle of the common man doing his work, his appointed work. It is the one thing in the universe which makes one fling expression to the winds and be satisfied simply to feel" (6:249). Simply to feel. Crane seems to feel about such men, perhaps mankind, the way some romantic and postmodern writers feel about the material universe. Here, too, lies one result of the Arnold-Huxley controversy of classical versus scientific education. Rejecting the notion of order provided by classicism and the romantic notion of the material world as beneficent, Crane is left with his feelings.

Crane's later work is both hurried and harried, filled with experiments not so much of craft but of feeling. If the craft is disappointing, as in many of the late war stories and especially in most of the *Tales of Whilomville*, that loss is occasionally paid for by advances in feeling and perception. Before Stevens demanded it, Crane had "become an ignorant man again." And if he did not see the sun clearly "in the idea of it," nevertheless, he was moving forward at the end.

In spite of his time's occasional economic depressions and constant social exploitation, Crane lived in an age and a country of unbounded optimism. At the same time, he was born, lived, and died in a world and a time when it was increasingly possible for people to deny utterly the existence of the supernatural and at the same time to disavow the ultimate value of mankind.

Only toward the end did he begin to find that value, and the literature of this century is still following the path Crane walked. Fewer than twenty years before the Great War, less than half a century from the atomic age, Crane struggled in a world where belief in God and man was rapidly unraveling at the seams; the mass, on the other hand, was in a frenzy of physical, verbal, and written motion to sew those seams, to shore fragments against its ruin. Alone, unwilling to compromise, unable to find solace anywhere, Stephen Crane stared at the gaping holes in the world's fabric, saw through them the abyss, and searched there for patches.

Notes

Preface

1 H. G. Wells, "Stephen Crane from an English Standpoint," *North American Review* 171 (August, 1900): 233–42; reprinted in *Stephen Crane's Career: Perspectives and Evaluations*, ed. Thomas A. Gullason (New York: New York University Press, 1972), pp. 126–33.

2 Joan Webber, *Milton and His Epic Tradition* (Seattle and London: University of Washington Press, 1979).

3 Cecil M. Bowra, *From Virgil to Milton* (London: Macmillan & Co., 1945), p. 246.

4 Warren D. Anderson, "Homer and Stephen Crane," *Nineteenth-Century Fiction* 19 (June, 1964): 77–86.

5 Robert Dusenbery, "The Homeric Mood of *The Red Badge of Courage*," *Pacific Coast Philology* 23 (April, 1968): 31–37.

6 Donald B. Gibson, "Crane's *The Red Badge of Courage*," *Explicator* 24 (February, 1966): item 49.

7 Sister Mary Anthony Weinig, "Homeric Convention in 'The Blue Hotel,'" *Stephen Crane Newsletter* 2 (Spring, 1968): 6–8.

8 Daniel Hoffman, *The Poetry of Stephen Crane* (New York and London: Columbia University Press, 1956; Columbia paperback ed., 1971). Frank Bergon, *Stephen Crane's Artistry* (New York and London: Columbia University Press, 1975).

9 Gilbert Highet, *The Classical Tradition: Greek and Roman Influences on Western Literature* (New York and London: Oxford University Press, 1949), p. vii.

10 Northrop Frye, *Anatomy of Criticism: Four Essays* (Princeton: Princeton University Press, 1957).

11 Sergio Perosa, "Naturalism and Impressionism in Stephen Crane's Fiction," in *Stephen Crane: A Collection of Critical Essays*, ed. Maurice Bassan (Englewood Cliffs, N. J.: Prentice-Hall, 1967), pp. 81–85; R. W. Stallman, *Stephen Crane: A Biography*, rev. ed. (New York: George Braziller, 1973), pp. 335–37 et passim; Donald B. Gibson, *The Fiction of Stephen Crane* (Carbondale, Ill.: Southern Illinois University Press, 1968); Thomas A. Gullason, introduction to *The Complete Short Stories and Sketches of Stephen Crane*, ed. Thomas A. Gullason (New York: Doubleday, 1963); Joseph Katz, introduction to *The Portable Stephen Crane*, ed. Joseph Katz (New York: Viking, 1969); Marsden La France, *A Reading of Stephen Crane* (London and New York: Oxford University Press, 1971); Milne Holton, *Cylinder of Vision: The Fiction and Journalistic Writing of Stephen Crane* (Baton Rouge: Louisiana State University Press, 1972); Jean Cazamajou, *Stephen Crane (1871–1900): Ecrivain Journaliste*, Etudes Anglaises, no. 35 (Paris: Librairie Didier, 1969); J. C. Levenson, introductions to vols. 2, 3, 4, 5, 7 of *The University of Virginia Edition of the Works of Stephen Crane*, ed. Fredson Bowers, 10 vols. (Charlottesville: The University Press of Virginia, 1969–76) (hereafter cited as *Works*; volume and page references in the text are to this edition); Bergon, *Crane's Astistry*; James Nagel, *Stephen Crane and Literary Impressionism* (University Park, Pa: Pennsylvania State University Press, 1980).

12 M. Solomon [pseud.], "Stephen Crane, A Critical Study," *Masses and Mainstream* 9, nos. 1 and 2 (January–March, 1956): 25–42, 31–47.

13 Thomas Beer, *Stephen Crane: A Study in American Letters* (Garden City, N. J.: Garden City Publishing Co., 1927), p. 359.

14 Fredric Jameson, *The Political Unconscious: Narrative as a Socially Symbolic Act* (Ithaca, N.Y.: Cornell University Press, 1981), p. 188; see also Raymond Williams, *The Country and the City* (New York: Oxford University Press, 1973), pp. 222–24.

15 Holton, *Cylinder of Vision*, p. 282.

Chapter One

1 James E. Miller, Jr., *The American Quest for a Supreme Fiction: Walt Whitman's Legacy in the Personal Epic* (Chicago and London: University of Chicago Press, 1979), p. 24; Miller is preceded in expressing this notion by Roy Harvey Pearce in *The Continuity of American Poetry* (Princeton: Princeton University Press, 1961) and others.

2 *Works*, 10:27.

3 An example: Rev. J. K. Peck, *Luther Peck and His Five Sons* (New York: Eaton & Main, 1897)—a book by a Peck about Pecks and their heroic efforts in converting the whole of western New York to Christianity. Interestingly, the book contains at least seven classical allusions; in one of which Achilles provides the odious side of a comparison with one of Luther's sons. Other examples: Bishop Peck wrote *What Must I Do to Be Saved?* (1848), and Stephen's father damns drink, dancing, novel reading, and the doctrine of infant damnation in *Essay on Dancing* (1848), *Popular Amusements* (1869), *Parts of Intoxication* (1870), and *Holiness the Birthright of All God's Children* (1874).

4 R. W. Stallman and Lillian Gilkes, *Stephen Crane: Letters* (New York: New York University Press, 1960), p. 242 (hereafter cited as *Letters*).

5 Beer, *Crane: A Study*, p. 106.

6 John Berryman, *Stephen Crane* (Cleveland and London: World Publishing Co., 1950), p. 21.

7 *Letters*, p. 8.

8 See Sidney Mead, "American Protestantism since the Civil War: From Denominationalism to Americanism," *Journal of Religion* 36 (January, 1956): 1.

9 *Letters*, pp. 42–43; *Works*, 7:51.

10 Stallman, *Biography*, p. 21.

11 Beer, *Crane: A Study*, p. 197.

12 *Letters*, p. 133.

13 From "In the Depths of a Coal Mine," *Works*, 8:605. The passage cited here is from a preliminary draft of the article which appeared in *McClure's*. It seems that the passage was so politically unsettling that either Crane himself or someone at *McClure's* struck this passage, or much of it, before the article was published.

14 Berryman, *Stephen Crane*, p. 277.

15 *Letters*, p. 60.

16 Ibid., p. 110.

17 Berryman, *Stephen Crane*, p. 252.

18 Stallman, *Biography*, passim.

19 Eric Solomon, *Stephen Crane: From Parody to Realism* (Cambridge, Mass.: Harvard University Press, 1966).

20 Also, Roy Harvey Pearce and J. Hillis Miller in *The Act of the Mind* (Baltimore: The Johns Hopkins University Press, 1965) have provided insights into the heroic immensely helpful in this study.

21 Aristotle, *Poetics*; "Longinus," *On the Sublime*, trans. W. Hamilton Fyfe (Cambridge, Mass.: Harvard University Press; London: Heinemann, 1965; Loeb Classical Library, 1st ed., 1927).

22 Wells, "Crane from an English Standpoint," in Gullason, *Crane's Career*, p. 133.

23 Stallman, *Biography*, p. 19.

24 Peck, *Luther Peck*, p. 108.

25 Stallman, *Biography*, p. 660.

26 Lyndon Upton Pratt, "The Formal Education of Stephen

Crane," *American Literature* 10 (January, 1939): 460–71.

27 *Letters*, p. 111.

28 Berryman, *Stephen Crane*, p. 183.

29 Petronius, *Satyricon*, trans. Michael Heseltine, rev. by E. H. Warmington (Cambridge, Mass.: Harvard Univeristy Press; London: Heinemann, 1959), "Poems," p. 409.

30 E. M. W. Tillyard, *The Epic Strain in the English Novel* (Fairlawn, N.J.: Essential Books, 1958), p. 16.

31 Stallman, *Biography*, p. 10.

32 Sculley Bradley et al., eds., *The American Tradition in Literature* (New York: W. W. Norton, 1962), p. 2; rev. ed., p. 816; Recast from R. W. Stallman, *Stephen Crane: An Omnibus* (New York: Knopf, 1952).

33 See James D. Conway, "The Stephen Crane–Amy Leslie Affair: A Reconsideration," *Journal of Modern Literature* 7 (February, 1979): 3–14. Once thought to have loved women one at time, Crane is convicted by his own hand of having two-timed Cora and Amy.

34 *Letters*, p. 300.

35 See Ernest L. Tuveson, *Redeemer Nation* (Chicago and London: University of Chicago Press, 1968), pp. 32–34 et passim.

36 *North American Review* 6 (November, 1818): 36–37.

37 Reprinted in R. W. Stallman, "Stephen Crane and Cooper's Uncas," *American Literature* 39 (November, 1967): 393–96; *Stephen Crane: Sullivan County Tales and Sketches* (Ames, Iowa: Iowa State University Press, 1968); *Works*, 8:199–201.

38 Leonard Lutwack, *Heroic Fiction: The Epic Tradition and American Novels of the Twentieth Century* (Carbondale, Ill.: Southern Illinois University Press, 1971), pp. 5–7.

39 Crane wrote a more obvious and simple mockery of the Horatio Alger fable in "A Self-Made Man: An Example of Success That Anyone Can Follow," *Works*, 8:124–29.

40 Miller, *American Quest*, pp. 13–29.

41 *Letters*, p. 86.

42 Among the best works in this area is Webber's *Milton and His Epic Tradition*. See especially chap. 1, "The Tradition."

43 See not only Jung, but Webber (pp. 12–13) and Erich Neumann, *The Origins and History of Consciousness*, trans. R. F. Hull (Princeton: Princeton University Press, 1973), p. 14; Joan Singer, *Boundaries of the Soul: The Practice of Jung's Psychology* (Garden City, N.Y.: Doubleday, 1972).

44 In spite of or perhaps because of its sexual overtones, the cave scene with Dido and Aeneas (bk. 4) provides a more famous example of this archetype.

45 The dark woods as archetype is much used in American literature up to the present century. Interestingly, since the trees have been cut down, many modern and postmodern American poets and writers have begun to use the vast open spaces of the West and Southwest as a wilderness archetype. Attitudes towards the wilderness archetype have also changed.

46 By "prototype" I mean the three essential qualities of epic are present in the story but not much more. The term bears a slight relationship to what Aristotle calls in the *Poetics* the "universal form" of epic. By this Aristotle means what is left of an epic after its various "episodes" have been re-moved.

47 Holton, *Cylinder of Vision*, passim.

48 Gibson, "Crane's *Red Badge*," item 49.

49 See, for example, LaFrance, *A Reading of Stephen Crane*, p. 76.

50 By the time of the *Aeneid*, "caves are enclosed violence" and include "the Trojan horse, the cave of Aeolus, Aetna, Allecto's cave"; Webber, *Epic Tradition*, p. 17.

51 Holton, *Cylinder of Vision*, p. 9.

52 *Works*, 8:xxxvi.

53 William James, "Reflex Action and Theism," in *The Will to Believe and Other Essays in Popular Philosophy* (New York: Dover, 1956), pp. 118–119—originally an address, but subsequently published in the *Unitarian Review* for October, 1881.

Chapter Two

1 Wallace Stevens, "[Prose statement on the poetry of war]," in *The Palm at the End of the Mind: Selected Poems and a Play*, ed. Holly Stevens (New York: Vintage Books, 1972), p. 206.

2 "Of the Origin of Homer and Hesiod, and Their Contest," in *Hesiod: The Homeric Hymns and Homerica*, trans. Hugh G. Evelyn-White (Cambridge, Mass.: Harvard University Press; London: Heinemann, 1967), Loeb Classical Library, pp. 565–97.

3 E. B. Castle, *Ancient Education and Today* (Baltimore: Penguin, 1961), p. 12; H. D. F. Kitto, *The Greeks* (Baltimore: Penguin, 1966), pp. 171–72.

4 Bowra, *From Virgil to Milton*, pp. 229–30.

5 M. Solomon [pseud.], "Crane, A Critical Study," p. 35.

6 R. W. Stallman, introduction to *The Red Badge of Courage* (New York: Random House, 1951), p. xxxv.

7 LaFrance, *A Reading of Stephen Crane*, pp. 100–101.

8 Cf. *Paradise Lost*, bks. 9–12, and Genesis, chap. 3. In both, a pattern of sin-guilt-alienation-repentance-promise of redemption is followed.

9 John E. Hart, "*The Red Badge of Courage* as Myth and Symbol," *University of Kansas City Review* 19 (Summer, 1953): 253; see also Joseph Campbell, *The Hero with a Thousand Faces* (Princeton: Princeton University Press, 1949), p. 30, for a discussion of heroes and hills.

10 Holton, *Cylinder of Vision*, pp. 5–11; Nagel, *Stephen Crane*

and Literary Impressionism, pp. 1–35.

11   The problems of authorial or narrative veracity *versus* Henry's (or Crane's or other narrators') "dramatic impressionism" (Holton's phrase) or narrative "parallax" (Nagel's) are involved and many. Suffice it that here basic action and direct speech are usually "fact," and that in the above instance, because Henry is hurt and temporarily speechless, all information comes from the narrator.

12   Gibson, "Crane's *Red Badge*," item 49.

13   But see William P. Safrenek, "Crane's *The Red Badge of Courage*," *Explicator* 26 (November, 1967): item 21. Failing to note the difference between running from and remaining in the battle, Safrenek sees Henry's development as paralleling Wilson's.

14   Although Crane was familiar with real "panthers" (actually eastern mountain lions), he would not have missed this allusion to a standard Christian epithet for Christ.

15   This vision differs from the Christian-group notion of man's insignificance because the latter then attaches man to something that *is* significant; the existential and in some ways Lucretian vision of man as an "insignificant thing" is probably closer to Henry's vision here.

16   Stevens, "[Prose statement]," p. 206.

17   Lucretius, *The Way Things Are*, trans. Rolfe Humphries (London and Bloomington: Indiana University Press, 1969). In book 1, Lucretius explains that men fear death because religion tells them to fear the eternal punishment of their immortal (albeit pagan) souls for their sins. Since neither body nor soul is immortal, man has nothing to fear from death.

18   The pertinent works are these: Henry Binder, "*The Red Badge of Courage* Nobody Knows," *Studies in the Novel* 10 (Spring, 1978): 9–47; *The Red Badge of Courage* and introduction by Henry Binder in *The Norton Anthology of American*

Literature, ed. Ronald Gottesman et al., 2 vols. (New York and London: Norton, 1979), 2:800–906; Henry Binder, "Unwinding the Riddle of Four Missing Papers from *The Red Badge of Courage*," *Publications of the Bibliographical Society of America* 72 (January–March, 1978): 100–106; Donald Pizer, "'*The Red Badge of Courage* Nobody Knows': A Brief Rejoinder," *Studies in the Novel* 11 (Spring, 1979): 77–81; Henry Binder, "Donald Pizer, Ripley Hitchcock, and *The Red Badge of Courage*," *Studies in the Novel* 11 (Summer, 1979): 216–23.

19 *Norton Anthology*, 2:854.
20 Ibid., p. 856.
21 For a smattering of the considerable body of opinion on this, see James Tuttleton, "The Imagery of *The Red Badge of Courage*," *Modern Fiction Studies* 8 (Winter, 1962): 411; C. C. Walcutt, *American Literary Naturalism: A Divided Stream* (Minneapolis: University of Minnesota Press, 1956), pp. 66–88, 223; Kermit Vanderbuilt and Daniel Weiss, "From Rifleman to Flagbearer: Henry Fleming's Separate Peace in *The Red Badge of Courage*," *Modern Fiction Studies* 11 (Winter, 1965–66): 371–80; Winifred Lynsky, ed., *Reading Modern Fiction*, 4th ed. (New York: Scribner's, 1968), pp. 173–77; Norman Friedman, "Criticism and the Novel," *Antioch Review* 18 (Fall, 1958): 343–70; Binder, "*The Red Badge of Courage* Nobody Knows," p. 9; most important is R. B. Sewall, "Crane's *The Red Badge of Courage*," *Explicator* 3 (May, 1945): item 55, along with Steven Mailloux, "*The Red Badge of Courage* and Interpretive Conventions: Critical Response to a Maimed Text," *Studies in the Novel* 10 (Spring, 1978): 48–63.
22 Some see Homer and Virgil as mocking their own ideals of heroism. Virgil, for example, may be said to have betrayed *pietas* and Roman stoicism by ending the *Aeneid* with Aeneas's impassioned killing of Turnus. Even Lucretius

seems to be horrified by the materialistic universe and its power to inflict pain and suffering as reflected in book 6 of *De rerum natura*.

23 Castle, *Ancient Education*, p. 12.

24 Given the moral heritage of most readers of Crane, even today, it is important to mention again that Crane felt there was "no such thing as sin, except in Sunday school." Beer, *Crane: A Study*, p. 106.

Chapter Three

1 *Letters*, p. 87.

2 Aristotle, *Poetics*.

3 Thomas A. Gullason, "Tragedy and Melodrama in Stephen Crane's *Maggie*," in *Stephen Crane: Maggie, a Girl of the Streets*, ed. Thomas A. Gullason, Norton Critical Edition (New York and London: Norton, 1979), pp. 245–53. Gullason sees in *Maggie* "a limited sense of Aristotelian tragedy," appeals to "pity and fear," and a "compact, dramatic, and scenic structure." What he calls the "tragic situation" of inequality in America is not "tragic," however shameful it might be. There is more of classical tragedy in *Maggie* than even Gullason seems to think is there.

4 Eric Solomon, *Crane: From Parody to Realism*, p. 23.

5 Ovid, *Metamorphoses*, bk. 5, lines 341–570. Since Ovid's account is used here, I use the Roman names for the gods in discussing *Maggie*.

6 A remarkable parallel to *Maggie* occurs in Puccini's *La Bohème*, the libretto for which was written in 1896. The heroine, Mimi, is similarly poor, forced to prostitute herself, and associated with flowers in the midst of the urban squalor of Paris. Further, both *La Bohème* and *Maggie* are naturalistic works which work hard at exposing the pathos of unrealistic perceptions of life. Unlike *Maggie*, however,

La Bohème is apparently based on a minor French novel written in 1844.

7 Holton, *Cylinder of Vision*, p. 53.

8 Gullason, "Tragedy and Melodrama," p. 245.

9 Holton, *Cylinder of Vision*, p. 43.

10 J. C. Levenson, introduction to *Works*, 7:xv.

11 Lyle D. Linder, " 'The Ideal and the Real' and 'Brer Washington's Consolation': Two Little-Known Stories by Stephen Crane," *American Literary Realism* 11, no. 1 (1978): 1–33.

12 Ralph Ellison, "Stephen Crane and the Mainstream of American Fiction," in Ellison's *Shadow and Act* (New York: Random House, 1953), pp. 60–76; on p. 75; Ellison speaks of *The Monster* as expressing "a violence of disgust with man and his condition." Crane's story has much in common, as well, with Ellison's *Invisible Man*.

13 Robert Barnes, "Stephen Crane's 'The Bride Comes to Yellow Sky,' " *Explicator* 16 (April, 1958): item 39; Kenneth Bernard, " 'The Bride Comes to Yellow Sky': History as Elegy," *English Review* 17 (April, 1967): 17–20; Scott C. Ferguson, "Crane's 'The Bride Comes to Yellow Sky,' " *Explicator* 21 (March, 1963): item 59.

14 O. Henry, *Heart of the West*, authorized ed. (New York: Doubleday, Page & Co., 1904), pp. 301–13 (page references in text are to this edition); for dating the events of this story, see Joseph Gallegly, *From Alamo Plaza to Jack Harris's Saloon* (The Hague, Paris: Mouton, 1970), pp. 151ff.

15 Eugene Current-Garcia. *O. Henry* (New York: Twayne, 1965).

16 Ben Merchant Vorpahl, "Murder by the Minute: Old and New in 'The Bride Comes to Yellow Sky,' " *Nineteenth-Century Fiction* 26 (September, 1971): 196–218.

17 Marvin Klotz, "Stephen Crane: Tragedian or Comedian:

'The Blue Hotel,'" *University of Kansas City Review* 27 (March, 1961): 170–74. Klotz feels that "The Blue Hotel" is a satire of the "naturalism–pessimistic determinism" fashionable in Crane's time. Such a view is entirely possible, given Crane's extremely inclusive art. If "The Bride" can have tragic possibilities within a larger framework of comedy, surely "The Blue Hotel" can entertain comic possibilities within a context of tragedy. In any event, Crane makes allowances for this when his narrator comments in "The Blue Hotel": "Any room can present a tragic front; any room can be comic" (5:156).

18 William H. Nolte, ed., *H. L. Mencken's "Smart Set" Criticism* (Ithaca, N.Y.: Cornell University Press, 1968), p. 295; Eric Solomon, *Crane: From Parody to Realism*, p. 257; Lynsky, *Reading Modern Fiction*, p. 173; Bruce L. Grenberg, "Metaphysics of Despair: Stephen Crane's 'The Blue Hotel,'" *Modern Fiction Studies* 14 (Summer, 1968): 203–13; Robert F. Gleckner, "Stephen Crane and the Wonder of Man's Conceit," *Modern Fiction Studies* 5 (Autumn, 1959): 271–81; Walter Sutton, "Pity and Fear in 'The Blue Hotel,'" *American Quarterly* 4 (Summer, 1952): 73–76.

19 *Letters*, p. 110.

20 George Chapman, *Bussy D'Ambois*, ed. Maurice Evans (New York: Hill and Wang, 1966). Cf. Crane in *Works*, 9:289: "The confusion was worse than in the mad night on the heath in *King Lear*"; also note "Poins and Falstaff congratulated themselves" (p. 392).

21 Weinig, "Homeric Convention."

22 Holton, *Cylinder of Vision*, p. 235: "In Crane true initiation rarely brings one into community and always involves more than just ritual. . . . the Swede achieves neither."

23 Weinig, "Homeric Convention," p. 7.

24 James Trammell Cox, "Stephen Crane as Symbolic Naturalist: An Analysis of 'The Blue Hotel,'" *Modern Fiction*

Studies 3 (Summer, 1957): 147–58.

25 Bruce A. Rosenberg, "Custer and the Epic of Defeat," *Journal of American Folklore* 88 (1974): 165–77.

26 Hugh N. Maclean, "The Two Worlds of 'The Blue Hotel,'" *Modern Fiction Studies* 5 (Autumn, 1959): 263.

27 See Stallman, *Biography*, p. 293; Eric Solomon, *Crane: From Parody to Realism*, p. 135–44; Levenson, introduction to *Works*, 3:xliii; Holton, *Cylinder of Vision*, p. 192.

28 The most important statements on this issue are set forth by Thomas Huxley's "Science and Culture" and Matthew Arnold's "Literature and Science." Interestingly, both men lectured on this and other issues in the United States in the 1870s and 1880s; it was a popular controversy.

29 Joseph Katz, "SC to Mrs. Moreton Frewen: A New Letter," *Stephen Crane Newsletter* 1 (Summer, 1967): 6.

Chapter Four

1 Gullason, "Tragedy and Melodrama," p. 245–53.

2 Kenneth T. Reed, "'The Open Boat' and Dante's *Inferno*: Some Undiscovered Analogues," *Stephen Crane Newsletter* 4 (Summer, 1970): 1–3; but see also Robert Meyers, "Crane's 'The Open Boat,'" *Explicator* 21 (April, 1963): item 60; Lloyd Dendinger, "Stephen Crane's Inverted Use of Key Images of 'The Rime of the Ancient Mariner,'" *Studies in Short Fiction* 5 (Winter, 1968): 192–94.

3 Donna Gerstenberger, "'The Open Boat': Additional Perspective," *Modern Fiction Studies* 17 (Winter, 1971–72): 558; but see also Bert Bender, "The Nature and Significance of 'Experience' in 'The Open Boat,'" *Journal of Narrative Technique* 9, no. 1 (1979): 70–79.

4 See not only Bender, but these: Robert Shulman, "Community, Perception, and the Development of Stephen Crane: *The Red Badge* to 'The Open Boat,'" *American Literature* 50 (November, 1978): 441–60; Joseph J. Kwait,

"Stephen Crane, Literary Reporter: Commonplace Experience and Artistic Transcendence," *Journal of Modern Literature* 8, no. 1 (1980): 129–38.

5 Clark Griffith, "Stephen Crane and the Ironic Last Word," *Philological Quarterly* 47 (January, 1968): 83–91.

6 Holton, *Cylinder of Vision*, p. 194.

7 Berryman, *Stephen Crane*, p. 183.

8 William K. Spofford, "Crane's *The Monster*," *Explicator* 36, no. 2 (1978): 5–7.

9 Eric Solomon, *Crane: From Parody to Realism*, p. 108.

10 Holton, *Cylinder of Vision*, p. 191.

11 Stallman, *Omnibus*, p. xxvi.

12 Stallman, *Omnibus*, and A. J. Liebling, "The Dollars Damned Him," *New Yorker*, August 5, 1961, pp. 48–60, 63–66, 69–72; see also Stallman, "That Crane, That Albatross around My Neck: A Self-Interview by R. W. Stallman," *Journal of Modern Literature* 7 (February, 1979): 147–69.

13 Charles Altieri, "From Symbolist Thought to Immanence: The Ground of Postmodern American Poetics," *Boundary* 2, 1 (Spring, 1973): 605.

14 Nagel, *Stephen Crane and Literary Impressionism*, p. 175.

15 Little Nell appears in "God Rest Ye, Merry Gentlemen" (6:136–54); Shackles in "God Rest Ye" and "The Revenge of the *Adolphus*" (6:155–71); Johnnie in "This Majestic Lie" (6:201–21); Vernall in "War Memories" (6:222–63).

16 Mere shock value, and perhaps some verisimilitude, comes from the following in "War Memories": "I remember Paine came ashore with a bottle of whiskey which I took from him violently" (6:227); Teddy Roosevelt, whom Crane knew, had called another Paine a "dirty little atheist"; but this passage was more probably addressed to a nation the majority of whose middle class spoke of drink as if it were as odious as murder.

17 From the *Lewiston* (Maine) *Journal* and reprinted in the *New York Tribune* (May 18, 1897); quoted in Stallman, *Biography*, p. 552. The *Buffalo Express* said a day earlier (also according to Stallman, *Biography*) that "Stephen Crane and Grover Cleveland are running a mad race in the use of the personal pronoun 'I,' with 'Steve' a neck ahead." The use of the "I" is of course not so much a measure of Crane's egotism as it is of his adherence to a credo of "personal honesty." It may also demonstrate that he is beginning to eschew the "impersonality" which characterizes modernism and coming closer to adopting the "personal" mode accepted by postmodernism. See also Bergon, *Crane's Artistry*.

18 John Killinger, *The Fragile Presence: Transcendence in Modern Literature* (Philadelphia: Fortress Press, 1973), p. 5.

19 Altieri, "Symbols of Thought," p. 612.

20 Ibid., p. 613.

21 Bergon, *Crane's Artistry*, p. 52.

22 *Letters*, p. 99.

Index